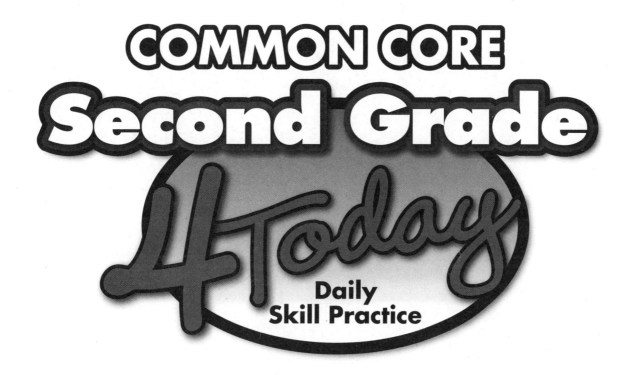

COMMON CORE
Second Grade
4Today
Daily Skill Practice

Grade 2

Carson-Dellosa Publishing, LLC
Greensboro, North Carolina

Credits

Content Editors: Christine Schwab, Angela Triplett
Proofreader: Julie B. Killian

 Visit *carsondellosa.com* for correlations to Common Core, state, national, and Canadian provincial standards.

Carson-Dellosa Publishing, LLC
PO Box 35665
Greensboro, NC 27425 USA
carsondellosa.com

ISBN 978-4838-1236-6
01-213141151

Table of Contents

Introduction

Common Core Second Grade 4 Today is a perfect supplement to the second-grade classroom curriculum. Students' skills will grow as they support their knowledge of math, language arts, science, and social studies with a variety of engaging activities.

This book covers 40 weeks of daily practice. Each day will provide students with cross-curricular content practice. During the course of four days, students complete questions and activities in math, language arts, science, and social studies in about 10 minutes. On the fifth day of each week, students complete a writing assessment that corresponds with one of the week's activities.

Various skills and concepts in math and language arts are reinforced throughout the book through activities that align to the Common Core State Standards. The standards covered for each week are noted at the bottom of each week's assessment page. For an overview of the standards covered, please see the Common Core State Standards Alignment Matrix on pages 5 to 8.

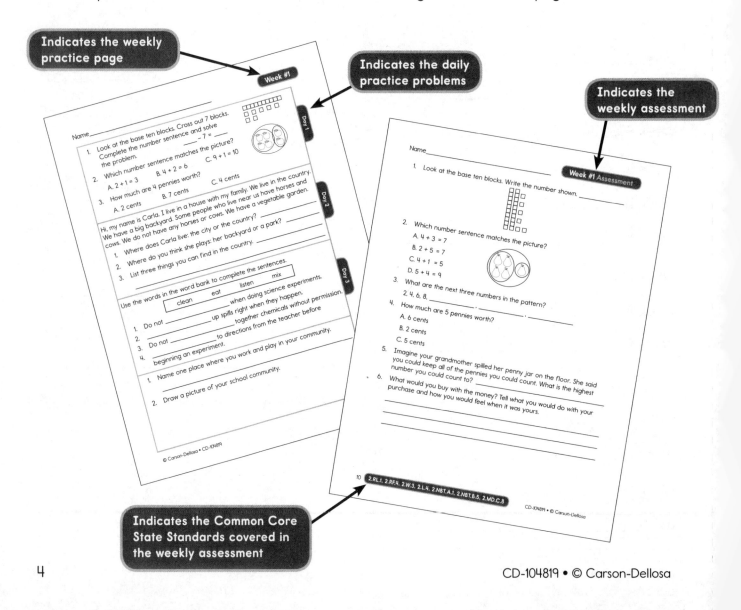

Indicates the weekly practice page

Indicates the daily practice problems

Indicates the weekly assessment

Indicates the Common Core State Standards covered in the weekly assessment

Language Arts

STANDARD	W1	W2	W3	W4	W5	W6	W7	W8	W9	W10	W11	W12	W13	W14	W15	W16	W17	W18	W19	W20
2.RL.1	•					•			•		•		•		•				•	
2.RL.2															•					
2.RL.3						•														
2.RL.4																				
2.RL.5																				
2.RL.6																				
2.RL.7																				
2.RL.9																				
2.RL.10																				
2.RI.1					•		•	•	•	•	•	•				•	•	•		
2.RI.2																	•			
2.RI.3						•														•
2.RI.4					•															
2.RI.5																		•		
2.RI.6																				
2.RI.7																				
2.RI.8																	•			
2.RI.9																				
2.RI.10							•										•			
2.RF.3		•	•	•				•		•	•	•	•	•	•					
2.RF.4	•				•	•	•		•		•		•		•		•		•	
2.W.1			•	•				•	•				•				•	•		•
2.W.2			•		•	•	•				•								•	
2.W.3	•	•										•		•	•	•				
2.W.5					•		•			•		•		•						
2.W.6																•			•	
2.W.7						•			•								•			
2.W.8										•										
2.SL.1							•		•											
2.SL.2																				
2.SL.3																				
2.SL.4																				
2.SL.5																				
2.SL.6																				
2.L.1								•	•		•	•				•		•		•
2.L.2		•		•				•		•								•		•
2.L.3		•		•				•		•							•	•		•
2.L.4	•				•				•		•	•		•	•	•	•			
2.L.5		•	•															•		
2.L.6					•				•	•							•			

W = Week

Common Core State Standards Alignment Matrix

Language Arts

STANDARD	W21	W22	W23	W24	W25	W26	W27	W28	W29	W30	W31	W32	W33	W34	W35	W36	W37	W38	W39	W40
2.RL.1	•							•	•		•		•							•
2.RL.2													•							
2.RL.3								•			•									•
2.RL.4																				
2.RL.5																	•			
2.RL.6																				
2.RL.7																				
2.RL.9																				
2.RL.10												•								
2.RI.1			•				•								•			•	•	
2.RI.2															•					
2.RI.3		•																		
2.RI.4															•				•	
2.RI.5																				
2.RI.6																				
2.RI.7						•														
2.RI.8																				
2.RI.9																				
2.RI.10				•	•										•				•	
2.RF.3	•	•			•		•		•						•	•			•	
2.RF.4		•	•		•				•		•		•		•		•		•	•
2.W.1								•			•	•	•				•	•	•	
2.W.2				•			•		•						•	•				
2.W.3		•	•		•					•				•						•
2.W.5	•																			
2.W.6														•	•					
2.W.7						•														
2.W.8					•		•				•							•		
2.SL.1																				
2.SL.2																				
2.SL.3																				
2.SL.4																				
2.SL.5																				
2.SL.6																				
2.L.1				•		•		•		•		•		•		•				
2.L.2				•		•				•		•		•		•				
2.L.3																				
2.L.4	•	•	•		•				•								•	•	•	•
2.L.5																				
2.L.6								•	•										•	

W = Week

 CD-104819 • © Carson-Dellosa

Common Core State Standards Alignment Matrix

Math

STANDARD	W1	W2	W3	W4	W5	W6	W7	W8	W9	W10	W11	W12	W13	W14	W15	W16	W17	W18	W19	W20
2.OA.A.1			●		●		●	●		●				●			●	●		
2.OA.B.2					●															
2.OA.C.3			●				●		●					●	●					●
2.OA.C.4													●		●			●	●	
2.NBT.A.1	●		●					●	●											
2.NBT.A.2													●							●
2.NBT.A.3		●			●							●			●		●			
2.NBT.A.4										●	●					●			●	
2.NBT.B.5	●			●		●		●		●	●	●	●						●	
2.NBT.B.6																				
2.NBT.B.7																				
2.NBT.B.8																●	●			
2.NBT.B.9																				
2.MD.A.1		●		●																
2.MD.A.2																				
2.MD.A.3																				
2.MD.A.4																				
2.MD.B.5												●								
2.MD.B.6																				
2.MD.C.7									●							●				●
2.MD.C.8	●		●								●			●			●			
2.MD.D.9																				
2.MD.D.10						●	●													
2.G.A.1					●			●		●		●								
2.G.A.2																				
2.G.A.3																				

W = Week

Math

STANDARD	W21	W22	W23	W24	W25	W26	W27	W28	W29	W30	W31	W32	W33	W34	W35	W36	W37	W38	W39	W40
2.OA.A.1		●		●						●		●		●			●	●		●
2.OA.B.2																				
2.OA.C.3																				
2.OA.C.4					●				●										●	
2.NBT.A.1					●															
2.NBT.A.2													●		●	●				
2.NBT.A.3		●										●								●
2.NBT.A.4	●					●		●			●									
2.NBT.B.5	●						●										●		●	●
2.NBT.B.6	●		●	●						●			●							
2.NBT.B.7			●					●	●		●						●		●	
2.NBT.B.8										●						●				
2.NBT.B.9																				
2.MD.A.1				●						●										
2.MD.A.2																				
2.MD.A.3					●	●		●						●						
2.MD.A.4		●					●													
2.MD.B.5			●																	
2.MD.B.6			●						●											
2.MD.C.7						●		●					●							
2.MD.C.8					●		●		●							●				
2.MD.D.9																	●			
2.MD.D.10											●			●	●					
2.G.A.1																		●	●	
2.G.A.2																				
2.G.A.3												●	●			●				●

W = Week

CD-104819 • © Carson-Dellosa

1. Look at the base ten blocks. Cross out 7 blocks. Complete the number sentence and solve the problem.   _____ – 7 = _____

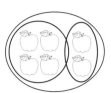

2. Which number sentence matches the picture?

   A. 2 + 1 = 3   B. 4 + 2 = 6   C. 9 + 1 = 10

3. How much are 4 pennies worth?

   A. 2 cents   B. 7 cents   C. 4 cents

Day 1

Hi, my name is Carla. I live in a house with my family. We live in the country. We have a big backyard. Some people who live near us have horses and cows. We do not have any horses or cows. We have a vegetable garden.

1. Where does Carla live: the city or the country? _____

2. Where do you think she plays: her backyard or a park? _____

3. List three things you can find in the country. _____

   _____

Day 2

Use the words in the word bank to complete the sentences.

clean	eat	listen	mix

1. Do not _____ when doing science experiments.

2. _____ up spills right when they happen.

3. Do not _____ together chemicals without permission.

4. _____ to directions from the teacher before beginning an experiment.

Day 3

---

1. Name one place where you work and play in your community.

   _____

2. Draw a picture of your school community.

Day 4

Name_____

1. Look at the base ten blocks. Write the number shown. _____

2. Which number sentence matches the picture?

    A. 4 + 3 = 7

    B. 2 + 5 = 7

    C. 4 + 1 = 5

    D. 5 + 4 = 9

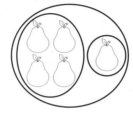

3. What are the next three numbers in the pattern?

    2, 4, 6, 8, _____ , _____ , _____

4. How much are 5 pennies worth?

    A. 6 cents

    B. 2 cents

    C. 5 cents

5. Imagine your grandmother spilled her penny jar on the floor. She said you could keep all of the pennies you could count. What is the highest number you could count to? _____

6. What would you buy with the money? Tell what you would do with your purchase and how you would feel when it was yours.

    _____

    _____

    _____

1. Fill in the missing numbers.

   7, _____, _____, 10

2. How long is the pencil? _____ cm

3. Write the number for each number word.

   one _____   three _____   five _____

Write the first word of the sentence with a capital letter.

1. (the) _____ flower smells nice.

Circle each picture whose name has a short vowel sound.

2.

Add an **-s** to the noun to make it plural. Write the new word on the line.

3. bird _____

Circle the best science tool to use in each situation.

1. observing a worm   microscope   hand lens   telescope
2. measuring how long it   thermometer   goggles   timer
   takes an ice cube to melt
3. adding very large   stopwatch   calculator   telescope
   numbers
4. keeping track of data   microscope   beaker   computer

Mia is a responsible citizen. She hangs up her book bag and jacket.
She turns in her homework on time. She is helpful to her friends. Mia is
respectful to her teachers.

1. Where is Mia a responsible citizen? _____

Jeff is a responsible citizen. He plants flowers at the park. He picks up trash.
He is helpful to his neighbors. Jeff volunteers at the local animal shelter.

2. Where is Jeff a responsible citizen? _____

Name_____

1. Write the first word of each sentence with a capital letter.

   (fruit) _____ is a good snack.

   (turn) _____ on the light, please.

   (yellow) _____ is my favorite color.

2. Circle each picture whose name has a short vowel sound.

3. Add an **-s** to each noun to make it plural. Write the new word on the line.

   skateboard _____   dinosaur _____

4. Imagine you saw a dinosaur in your backyard one morning. What would you do first? What would you do next? Write a story. Provide a conclusion. Use correct punctuation after your sentences.

   _____

   _____

   _____

   _____

   _____

   _____

   _____

   _____

   _____

   _____

   _____

   _____

   _____

   _____

2.RF.3, 2.W.3, 2.L.2, 2.L.3, 2.L.5, 2.NBT.A.3, 2.MD.A.1

1. Look at the base ten blocks.
   Write the number shown. _____

   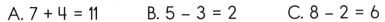

2. Which number sentence matches the picture?

   A. 7 + 4 = 11   B. 5 – 3 = 2   C. 8 – 2 = 6

3. Victor had 2 nickels. Shelby gave him 2 pennies. How much money does Victor have now? _____

1. Read or listen to the poem. Circle each letter **o** that makes the **short o** sound.

   Otter likes to play
   With many things
   Such as olives, octagons,
   And big, round rings.

2. What is an **octagon**?   A. number   B. shape   C. car

3. What month's name starts with the **short o** sound? _____

1. Circle the science tools that can be used for measuring.

   balance scale   test tube   ruler   magnet

   yardstick   stopwatch   hand lens   thermometer

2. Choose a tool you circled. Tell what it measures.

   _____

1. List a set of rules that will help your classroom be a good place to learn.

   The Constitution of Room _____

   _____

   _____

   _____

Name_____

1. Measure the length of a book with a paper clip. About how many paper clips long is it?

   _____ paper clips

2. Draw a balance scale. Draw something on both sides of the scale. Make sure the scale tilts correctly.

3. Write about three things you could do with a magnet. Then, tell why magnets are or are not good tools.

   _____

   _____

   _____

   _____

   _____

   _____

   _____

   _____

   _____

   _____

   _____

 2.RF.3, 2.W.1, 2.W.2, 2.L.5, 2.OA.A.1, 2.OA.C.3, 2.NBT.A.1, 2.MD.C.8

Name_____

1. How long is the key? _____ cm

2. What number does the cupcake represent? _____

    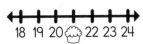

3. What number is 10 more than 12? _____

Write the first word of the sentence with a capital letter.

1. (where) _____ is your pen?

Circle each picture whose name has a short vowel sound.

2.

Add **-s** to the noun to make it plural. Write the new word on the line.

3. glove _____

1. What is something scientists may sort?

    _____

2. How might sorting be helpful to them?

    _____

    _____

The **past** is time gone by. The **present** is the time you live in now. The **future** is the time that has not happened yet.

1. Write **past**, **present**, or **future** beside each car.

2. Name one object from the past. _____

Name_____

_____   _____

1. Write **past** or **present** for each picture above.

2. What clues helped you decide how to label the pictures?

_____

_____

3. Would you want to live in the past, present, or future? Why?

_____

_____

_____

_____

_____

_____

_____

_____

_____

2.RF.3, 2.W.1, 2.L.2, 2.L.3, 2.NBT.B.5, 2.MD.A.1

1. Write the number word for each number.

   4 _____   10 _____   7 _____

2. Draw two different triangles.

3. Tara had 4 lollipops and gave 1 of them away. How many lollipops did she have left? Write a number sentence to show how you solved the problem. _____

4. 11 – 6 = _____   9 – 6 = _____   8 – 2 = _____

West Indian manatees live along the coast of Florida. They are shy and gentle. Manatees are herbivores. This means that they eat only plants. Baby manatees are called calves. They drink their mothers' milk as all mammals do.

1. Which word better describes a manatee: mean or sweet? _____

2. What is an herbivore? _____

3. What are baby manatees called? _____

Laura normally makes nachos in the microwave with tortilla chips and shredded cheddar cheese. Because she was out of cheddar, today she used mozzarella. Unfortunately, the cheese burned. This gave her an idea for a science experiment. She bought a third kind of cheese.

1. What question do you think she came up with?

   _____

   _____

A **right** is the freedom to do something. A **responsibility** is an action a person must take. Fill in the each blank with **right** or **responsibility**.

1. Students have the _____ to go to school. It is their _____ to do their best to learn.

2. Citizens have the _____ to live where they wish. They have the _____ to be good neighbors.

1. Write the number word for each number.

   9 _____   12 _____   8 _____

2. Marisa picked up 12 shells at the beach. She gave 6 shells to her brother. How many shells did Marisa have left? _____ shells

   Write a number sentence to show how you solved the problem.

   _____

3. Draw a flat shape that has no straight sides or angles.

4. Tell how to play a card game such as Go Fish. If you do not remember all of the steps, ask your teacher or another student for help. Use number words in your instructions.

   _____
   _____
   _____
   _____
   _____
   _____
   _____
   _____
   _____

 2.RI.1, 2.RI.4, 2.RF.4, 2.W.2, 2.W.5, 2.L.4, 2.L.6, 2.OA.A.1, 2.OA.B.2, 2.NBT.A.3, 2.G.A.1

Day 1

1. Look at the picture graph. How many scoops did all 3 children eat? _____ scoops

   Total Scoops of
   Ice Cream Eaten

Chase	🍦🍦🍦
Fiona	🍦🍦
Mandy	🍦

   🍦 = 1 scoop

2. Write <, >, or = to make each statement true.

   10 ◯ 12   33 ◯ 43   19 ◯ 19

3. Add or subtract mentally.

   52 + 10 = _____   44 – 10 = _____   20 + 10 = _____

Day 2

Mary Lou French sat on a bench,
Munching a sandwich and chips.
When a tarantula spied her and climbed up beside her,
She told him to take a long trip!

1. What characters are in this poem? _____

2. What is a tarantula: venomous spider or fuzzy kitten? _____

3. What is Mary Lou eating? _____

Day 3

1. Put the following sentences in the correct order for conducting a science experiment. Label them **1** to **5**.

   _____ Keep track of the results.

   _____ Decide what question you are trying to answer.

   _____ Write a conclusion that answers your question.

   _____ Gather materials.

   _____ Conduct the science experiment.

Day 4

In the early 1800s, Johnny Appleseed grew apple trees and gave apple seeds to pioneers in the midwestern part of the United States. One legend says that he carelessly threw his apple seeds along the sides of roads and along streams. He actually planted his seeds in just the right places along the countryside.

1. Name one legend about Johnny Appleseed. _____

   _____

2. Name one fact about Johnny Appleseed. _____

   _____

The early life of the green sea turtle is full of danger. After the mother turtle lays eggs in the sand, each baby uses an egg tooth to chip its way out of its egg. The mother turtle does not stay there to help. Each baby turtle must stay out of the way of crabs, coyotes, and dogs. The baby turtles hide in the sand until night. Then, they crawl to the sea.

1. What animals are in the passage? _____

2. How does each turtle get out of its egg? _____

3. Where do the turtles hide? _____

4. Animals have different ways of keeping safe. Use the Internet, books, or magazines to research and write a report about how one animal behaves to keep safe.

_____

_____

_____

_____

_____

_____

_____

_____

_____

_____

_____

_____

_____

_____

_____

1. Peter ate 4 grapes. Later, he ate 3 more grapes. How many grapes did Peter eat in all? _____ grapes

2. Write <, >, or = to make the statement true.   15 ◯ 25

3. Is the number of birds even or odd? _____

Marcus is a farmer. He has an important job. He grows food that we eat. Marcus grows wheat and oats. He also takes care of the animals on his farm. Marcus works hard. He gets up early every day. He works until it is dark.

1. Who is this story about? _____

2. What does he do for a job? _____

3. What does he farm?   plants   animals   both

Students in Pablo's class took a survey on their transportation to school. Here are the results:

How We Get to School				
walk: 6	bus: 11	car: 4	bike: 2	other: 2

1. Discuss with a partner ways you could organize and display the data. What are two ways you came up with?

    _____

A **dictionary** gives you the spelling, pronunciation, and meaning of words. A **thesaurus** lists words with their synonyms and antonyms. An **atlas** is a book of charts, maps, and tables.
Circle the best way to find the following information:

1. meaning of the word **reign**   atlas   dictionary

2. countries in South America   thesaurus   atlas

3. another word for **huge**   atlas   thesaurus

Number of Caterpillars Second-
Grade Classes Saw at the Park

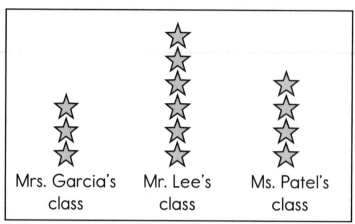

⭐ = 2 caterpillars

1. Which class found the fewest caterpillars? _____

2. Which class found the most caterpillars? _____

3. How many caterpillars did the three classes find in all?

   _____ caterpillars

4. Write a report to tell how a caterpillar becomes a butterfly. Show your
   report to your teacher. Make changes if needed. Then, type your report
   on a computer.

   _____

   _____

   _____

   _____

   _____

   _____

   _____

   _____

   _____

**2.RI.1, 2.RI.10, 2.RF.4, 2.W.2, 2.W.5, 2.SL.1,
2.OA.A.1, 2.OA.C.3, 2.MD.D.10**

CD-104819 • © Carson-Dellosa

1. Write the number that is 6 tens and 8 ones. _____

2. Circle the shapes that have 4 sides.

3. Perry ran 7 laps at the gym on Saturday. On Sunday, he ran 8 laps at the gym. How many laps did Perry run at the gym all weekend? _____ laps

Circle the letters that should be capitalized.

1. tyler's birthday is november 4.

Underline the verb in the sentence.

2. We eat pizza for lunch.

Create your own question. Remember to add correct punctuation.

3. What _____

1. Look closely at your hand, palm-side up. Write five things you observe about your palm. Underline the adjectives.

_____

_____

_____

_____

Christopher Columbus was an Italian explorer. In August of 1492, he sailed west from Spain with three ships. The ships were named the *Niña*, the *Pinta*, and the *Santa Maria*. In October of 1492, he landed on a small island called San Salvador.

1. Who was Christopher Columbus? _____

2. What were the names of the three ships?

_____ _____ _____

There were many jobs on Christopher Columbus's ships. Crewmen could mend the sails and ropes or move the sails. Another job was cooking for the passengers. A crewman could also be the lookout at the front of the ship.

1. If you were a crewman on one of the ships, which job would you want to have? Why?

   _____

   _____

   _____

2. Would you want to sail on a voyage to an unknown place as Christopher Columbus did? Why or why not? Give reasons to support your opinion.

   _____

   _____

   _____

   _____

   _____

   _____

   _____

   _____

   _____

   _____

   _____

Name_____

1. Look at the base ten blocks. Write the number shown. _____

2. Is the number of leaves even or odd? _____

3. What time is shown? _____

Barker wished she was the biggest dog on the block. Every time Barker saw Bruiser, she hung her head. "I'll never be that big," she thought. "What good is a little dog? A big dog can carry newspapers. She can chase away pesky cats."

1. Write a compound word from the passage. _____

2. Is Barker happy or jealous? _____

3. What does Barker wish? _____

    _____

1. Use the following properties to describe a mystery object. Then, read your answers to a partner and have him try to figure out what it is.

    size _____ color _____ temperature _____

    weight _____ texture _____ magnetism _____

2. What was your mystery object? _____

3. Was your partner able to guess what it was? _____

Read each problem. Then, write a solution. Share your solutions with a partner. Does she agree or disagree with you?

1. School has been delayed for two hours, but the adults in your home must go to work on time. _____

    _____

2. A classmate wants to copy your homework. _____

    _____

1. Look at the base ten blocks. Write the number shown. _____

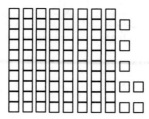

2. Is the number of eggs even or odd? _____

3. What time is shown? _____

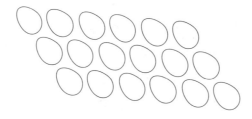

4. What is your favorite time of day? Give reasons to support your opinion.

_____

_____

_____

_____

2.RL.1, 2.RI.1, 2.RF.4, 2.W.1, 2.SL.1, 2.L.1, 2.L.4, 2.L.6, 2.OA.C.3, 2.NBT.A.1, 2.MD.C.7

Name_____

Day 1

1. Write the number 83 in expanded form. _____

2. How many sides does a pentagon have? _____

3. Mario picks 28 flowers. Nora picks 16 flowers. How many more flowers does Mario pick than Nora? Write a number sentence to show how you solved the problem. _____

4. 17 − 6 = _____   17 + 3 = _____

Day 2

Circle the letters that should be capitalized. Add punctuation.

1. Is soccer practice on thursday

Underline the verb in the sentence.

2. The bunny hops.

Add **-es** to the noun to make it plural. Write the new word on the line.

3. watch _____

Day 3

1. Name the three states of matter. Give an example of each.

_____

_____

_____

Day 4

Jackie Joyner-Kersee is a great athlete. She was an Olympic track star. She was born in 1962. In 1981, she started training for her first Olympics. She won a silver medal in her first Olympic competition in 1984. She went on to win a gold medal in the 1988 Olympics and a bronze medal in the 1992 Olympics. She has held the American long jump record for more than 15 years.

1. Create a time line to show Jackie Joyner-Kersee's accomplishments.

_____

1. Circle the letters that should be capitalized.

    our club meets every other saturday in july and august.

2. Underline the verb in each sentence.

    Malia swims after school.

    Josh plays basketball at the gym.

3. Underline the letter or letters at the end of each word that tell you how to make it plural. Write the new word on the line.

    mix _____   wish _____

4. Write a question you would like your classmates to answer. Remember to use correct punctuation.

    _____

5. After your classmates have answered your question, tell what you have learned. Show your report to the same classmates to see if you remembered everything. Make changes if needed.

    _____

    _____

    _____

    _____

    _____

    _____

    _____

    _____

    _____

    _____

    _____

    _____

 2.RI.1, 2.RF.3, 2.W.5, 2.W.7, 2.L.2, 2.L.3, 2.L.6, 2.OA.A.1, 2.NBT.A.4, 2.NBT.B.5, 2.G.A.1   CD-104819 • © Carson-Dellosa

1. Jared had 20 cents. He bought a piece of candy for 15 cents. How much money did Jared have left? _____ cents

2. Write **<**, **>**, or **=** to make each statement true.

   125 ◯ 116   54 ◯ 23   98 ◯ 98

3. 5 + _____ = 12   6 + _____ = 15   3 + _____ = 9

The clock showed midnight. Two mice sat in their home. They talked about the things they wanted to do. One wanted to eat all of the cheese in the world. The other wanted to break all of the mousetraps in the world.

1. Where does this story take place? _____

2. When does this story take place? _____

3. What do you call more than one mouse? _____

4. Do you think the mice can really do what they are talking about? ___

   Why or why not? _____

Unscramble the words to complete the sentences.

1. Water is a _____ (iqludi).

2. If it freezes, it becomes _____ (cei), which is a _____ (dislo).

3. If water is heated, it becomes _____ (trewa pavor), which is a _____ (sga).

American Indian tribes had different homes. Southwestern tribes used adobe bricks to keep the insides cool. People used ladders to get from one level to the next. Eastern Woodland tribes used branches and bark to make their longhouses. Plains tribes made tepee homes from poles and animal skins.

1. Write the name of each tribe below the correct house.

_____   _____   _____

Name_____

1. Use the words in the word bank to complete the paragraph about matter.

forms	gas	liquid	mass
see	solid	space	taste

    Everything you can _____ , smell, and _____ is
    matter. All matter takes up _____ and has _____ .
    Matter comes in three different _____ . Matter can be a
    _____ , a _____ , or a _____ .

2. Write about something you or someone you know did this week that made
    a physical change in some form of matter. Be sure to use the correct
    sequence of events.

    _____

    _____

    _____

    _____

    _____

    _____

    _____

    _____

    _____

    _____

    _____

    _____

    _____

    _____

    _____

    _____

    _____

    _____

 2.RL.1, 2.RI.1, 2.RF.3, 2.RF.4, 2.W.2, 2.W.8,
2.L.1, 2.L.4, 2.NBT.A.4, 2.NBT.B.5, 2.MD.C.8

Day 1

1. Write each number.   4 hundreds, 3 tens, 2 ones _____

   2 hundreds, 4 ones _____

2. Name this shape. _____ ☐

3. James is running a race that is 15 miles. He stops to eat an energy bar after running 11 miles. How many miles does James have left to run? _____ miles

Day 2

Circle the letters that should be capitalized.

1. wallace beck   ruby rossi

Write **C** next to each common noun. Write **P** next to each proper noun.

2. April _____   dog _____

Add the correct ending mark (**. ? !**) to the end of the sentence.

3. That bunny is so cute

Day 3

Use the words in the word bank to complete the sentences.

down	hill	pull	push	top

1. A ball is at the _____ of a hill.

2. If I _____ the ball, it will roll _____ the hill.

3. A wagon is at the bottom of a _____ .

4. If I _____ the wagon, it will go up the hill.

Day 4

Alexander Graham Bell was an inventor and scientist. He was born in Scotland in 1847. He is most famous for inventing the telephone in 1876. He and his friend Thomas Watson did many experiments with electricity before Bell invented the telephone.

1. What is Alexander Graham Bell most famous for? _____

2. What year did he invent the telephone? _____

3. What was his friend's name? _____

Alexander Graham Bell is most famous for inventing the telephone. He also did many other things. He taught music and speech. He created a research laboratory for the deaf. He invented an electric probe used by doctors. He worked on ways to locate icebergs by using echoes.

1. Use the graphic organizer to list some of the things Alexander Graham Bell did during his lifetime. Begin by writing his last name in the middle.

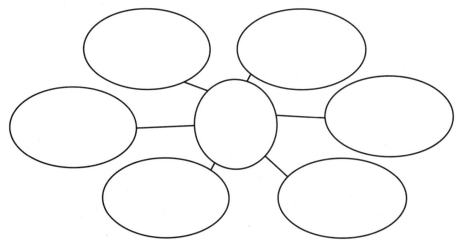

Before the invention of the telephone, it was harder to communicate with people who were far away. The telephone was a solution to the problem.

2. Think of a time you had a problem. How did you solve it? Include details to describe thoughts, feelings, or actions.

_____

_____

_____

_____

_____

_____

_____

_____

_____

_____

2.RI.1, 2.RF.3, 2.W.3, 2.W.5, 2.L.1, 2.L.4, 2.NBT.A.3, 2.NBT.B.5, 2.MD.B.5, 2.G.A.1

Day 1

1. Which equation matches the array?

   A. 4 + 4 + 4 = 12   B. 3 + 3 = 6   C. 5 + 5 + 5 + 5 = 20

2. Count by 10s.

   340, 350, 360, _____ , _____ , _____

3. 82 – 31 = _____   26 + 53 = _____

Day 2

The submarine moved deep in the ocean. Eric saw fish and an octopus outside the window. He looked at his watch. "It's so dark down here. It does not seem like four o'clock," he thought.

1. What time of day does this story take place? _____

2. When is that time of day?

   A. the afternoon   B. the middle of the night

3. Where does this story take place? _____

4. What does Eric see in this setting that he cannot see at home?

   _____

Day 3

Fill in the blanks to complete the sentences.

1. Gravity is a f___ rc___ that pulls objects toward E___ r___h.

2. Gravity keeps objects from flo___ t___ng away.

3. Give an example of gravity.

   _____

Day 4

A **culture** is when a group of people share the same clothes, music, and food. Members of a culture can live in the same area and speak the same language.

1. Draw a picture of people in your culture. Then, write a sentence to describe it.

   _____

Name_____

1. Which equation matches the array?

   A. 2 + 2 + 2 + 2 + 2 = 10

   B. 3 + 3 + 3 + 3 + 3 + 3 = 18

   C. 2 + 2 + 2 = 6

   D. 5 + 5 + 5 = 15

2. Count by 10s.

   250, 250, 260, _____ , _____ , _____

3. 56 + 32 = _____   95 – 61 = _____

4. Ty had 15 DVDs in his movie collection. He got 8 more for his birthday. How many DVDs does Ty have? _____ DVDs

5. Write about a movie you have seen. Include details about the story of the movie. Conclude with your opinion of the movie and whether you think others should watch it. Give reasons to support your opinion.

   _____

   _____

   _____

   _____

   _____

   _____

   _____

   _____

2.RL.1, 2.RF.3, 2.RF.4, 2.W.1, 2.OA.C.4, 2.NBT.A.2, 2.NBT.B.5   CD-104819 • © Carson-Dellosa

Name_____

1. Jimmy has 55 cents in his pocket. Draw the coins that Jimmy could have in his pocket.

2. 86 – 51 = _____

3. Is the number of lollipops even or odd? _____

Circle the letters that should be capitalized.

1. mr. george lewis   ms. ava novak

Write **C** next to each common noun. Write **P** next to each proper noun.

2. Pacific _____   lake _____

Add the correct ending mark (**. ? !**) to the end of the sentence.

3. My cat loves tuna

Circle the word that correctly completes each sentence.

1. A _____ can pick up many things made from metal.
   lightbulb   magnet   pencil

2. _____ is like a giant magnet.
   Earth   A tree   Water

3. A _____ always points north.
   telescope   compass   lightbulb

December has many different celebrations. Christmas, Hanukkah, and Kwanzaa are celebrated by families during this month.

1. Write the name of a holiday you celebrate in December. _____

2. Write two complete sentences about your celebration.

_____

_____

_____

1. Circle the letters that should be capitalized.

    dr. friedman   mrs. grace edwards   aunt cheryl

2. Write **C** next to each common noun. Write **P** next to each proper noun.

    _____ Mr. Ling   _____ bus stop   _____ Sara Conti

3. Add the correct ending mark (**. ? !**) to the end of each sentence.

    I am looking for my cat

    Will you help me look for my cat

    I cannot believe you found my cat

4. If you could cook a meal for your family, what would you make? Describe the meal and explain how to make it.

    _____

    _____

    _____

    _____

    _____

    _____

    _____

    _____

    _____

    _____

    _____

    _____

    _____

 2.RF.3, 2.W.3, 2.W.5, 2.L.4, 2.OA.A.1, 2.OA.C.3, 2.MD.C.8   CD-104819 • © Carson-Dellosa

1. Write an addition equation for the array.

    _____

2. Write the number word for each number.

    30 _____   61 _____   73 _____

3. Circle the dog that has an odd number of spots.

I can wiggle my tooth with my tongue. It is getting really loose! Today, I tried to eat an apple. My loose tooth made it **impossible**! It really hurt. My mom cut the apple into pieces for me.

1. Which word rhymes with **tongue**: song or sung? _____

2. What does **impossible** mean? _____

3. What is this story mostly about? _____

4. Underline one sentence that helped you answer question 3.

---

1. A candle's flame is an example of _____ energy.

    A. gravity   B. light   C. solar   D. sound

2. A rainbow is created by _____ energy.

    A. gravity   B. light   C. solar   D. sound

A **primary source** is a paper, object, or communication that comes from the subject a person is studying about. It can be a diary, speech, or interview. A primary source can also be a piece of clothing or furniture. A **secondary source** is used to explain or tell more about the primary source. Circle which source best describes the following:

1. movie about Martin Luther King Jr.   primary   secondary

2. interview with Barack Obama   primary   secondary

3. book about George Washington   primary   secondary

4. Abraham Lincoln's hat   primary   secondary

1. _____ gives us heat and light energy.

   A. A plant

   B. The sun

   C. The moon

   D. A magnet

2. Circle the forms of energy.

   sound   light   matter   heat   mass

3. Name two sources of energy you can use to cook food.

   _____   _____

4. Circle the names of the objects that need electricity to work.

   computer   car   microwave   bathtub   lamp

5. Imagine a big storm happens where you live. The electricity is not working. How will this change what you do in a day? How will you feel? Write a story. Type it on a computer.

   _____

   _____

   _____

   _____

   _____

   _____

   _____

   _____

   _____

   _____

   _____

Name_____

Day 1

1. Draw hands on the clock to show 12:30.

2. Write <, >, or = to make each statement true.

   203 ◯ 233   400 ◯ 300   555 ◯ 556

3. Write the number that is 10 more than each number.

   110 _____   620 _____   880 _____

Day 2

Read the book title. Rewrite the title with the correct capital letters.

1. *green eggs and ham* _____

Read the sentence. Circle the helping verb. Underline the main verb.

2. Jarvis can watch a movie with me tonight.

Read the sentence. Add commas where they are needed.

3. We study spelling math history and art.

Day 3

Use the words in the word bank to complete the sentences.

| ears | high | soft | vibrations |

1. Sounds are made from _____.

2. They can be loud or _____.

3. Sounds can be different pitches. Some are _____,
   and some are low.

4. We use our _____ to hear sounds.

Day 4

Chinese New Year is a holiday. It is celebrated in January or February. There is a colorful parade with a Chinese dragon. It dances in the street. It tries to catch money from the crowd. Families get together to watch fireworks.

1. When is Chinese New Year? _____

2. What dances in the street and tries to catch money? _____

   _____

3. What do families do during Chinese New Year? _____

   _____

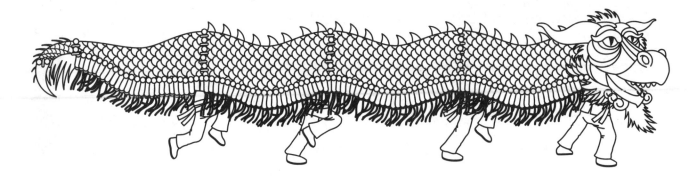

Read each sentence. Circle **fact** or **opinion**.

1. Chinese New Year is a holiday.   fact   opinion

2. The parade is fun.   fact   opinion

3. The food is wonderful.   fact   opinion

4. The dragon dances in the parade.   fact   opinion

5. Think about a time you went to a celebration. Maybe you went to a parade or saw fireworks. Maybe it was a special party. Write about it. Include details to describe thoughts, feelings, or actions.

_____

_____

_____

_____

_____

_____

_____

_____

_____

_____

_____

_____

_____

1. Write the expanded form of each number.

   230 _____   573 _____

2. Draw two ways to show 50 cents.

3. Write the number that is 100 less than each number.

   _____ 655   _____ 248   _____ 213

Many birds migrate south in the winter. They cannot find enough food where it is cold. They fly south where it is warm. There, they find food for the winter. When winter is over, they fly north.

1. Do all birds migrate south in the winter? _____

2. Place an **X** next to the main idea of this passage.
   _____ Birds migrate south so that they can find food.
   _____ When winter is over, birds fly north.

3. Write one detail that supports the main idea. _____

Draw a line to match each word with its definition.

1. flashlight   A. an arch of colors that often appears when the sun comes out after it has rained

2. mirror   B. a portable light source, often used during power outages

3. rainbow   C. a darker area caused by a blocked light source
                 D. a surface that reflects light well, often used to
4. shadow   see reflections

Technology changes things over time. Look at the pictures.

1. Name two things that have changed about the phone over time.

   _____

   _____

1. Write the expanded form of each number.

   466 _____   104 _____

2. Fill in the chart. Below each number, write the number that is 100 less.

152	638	216	436	722

3. Andrew sold 23 pizzas on Thursday. He sold 42 pizzas on Friday. How many pizzas did Antonio sell in all? _____ pizzas

4. What toppings do you like on your pizza? Ask three classmates about their favorite toppings. Write about a pizza you could make for all of you. Then, show your report to the same classmates to see if you remembered everything. Make changes if needed.

   _____

   _____

   _____

   _____

   _____

   _____

   _____

   _____

   _____

 2.RI.1, 2.RI.2, 2.RI.8, 2.RI.10, 2.RF.4, 2.W.1, 2.W.7, 2.L.4, 2.L.6, 2.OA.A.1, 2.NBT.A.3, 2.NBT.B.8, 2.MD.C.8   CD-104819 • © Carson-Dellosa

1. Write an addition equation for the array.

    _____

2. A chef cracked 19 eggs. A few minutes later, he cracked 3 more eggs. How many eggs did the chef crack in all?

    _____ eggs

Read the title. Rewrite the title with the correct capital letters.

1. *the big book of lizards* _____

Read the sentences. Circle the helping verbs. Underline the main verbs.

2. Amy will write her report after class.

3. The bird can fly south.

4. The sun will rise tomorrow.

Write **L** for each object that is living. Write **N** for each object that is nonliving.

1. _____ cat   2. _____ paper

3. _____ snow   4. _____ rock

5. _____ clock   6. _____ car

7. _____ tree   8. _____ zebra

The Statue of Liberty stands on an island in New York Harbor. France gave the statue to the United States as a gift to celebrate the friendship between the two countries. It is a symbol of **opportunity**. The statue has welcomed many people who have come to the United States looking for a better life.

1. What does **opportunity** mean? _____

    _____

2. Who gave the statue to the United States? _____

1. Read the sentences. Circle the helping verbs. Underline the main verbs.

   Molly will ride the evening bus.

   The squirrels can find food now.

2. Read the magazine title. Rewrite the title with the correct capital letters.
   dog fancy

   _____

3. Read the book title. Rewrite the title with the correct capital letters.
   the horse that spoke spanish

   _____

4. Choose and read a book from the class library. Write a report about it. Include what you think of the book. Give reasons to support your opinion. Be sure to write the title and the name of the author.

   _____

   _____

   _____

   _____

   _____

   _____

   _____

   _____

   _____

   _____

1. 62 + 34 = _____

2. Write <, >, or = to make each statement true.

   230 ◯ 203   37 ◯ 370   405 ◯ 405

3. Draw an array for the equation.

   2 + 2 + 2 = 6

"Did you hear that noise?" asked Ellen.

"What was it?" asked Avery.

The girls pulled their sleeping bags up to their chins. Their hands shook with fright as they listened in the darkness.

1. Who is in this story? _____

2. What time of day might it be?

   A. 10 o'clock am   B. 10 o'clock pm

3. How do the girls feel? _____

---

1. Write **yes** or **no** to complete the chart.

   ### What Do Plants and Animals Need?

	light	water	air	shelter
plants				
animals				

2. What do both plants and animals need?

   _____

At the top of the globe is the North Pole.
At the bottom is the South Pole.
The equator is the imaginary line that
runs east and west and divides Earth.

1. Label the **North Pole**, **South Pole**,
   and **equator** on the globe.

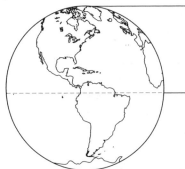

---

1. Both plants and animals need _____ to live.

   A. space   B. shelter   C. water

2. Animals _____ to get their food.

   A. shop   B. hunt   C. cook

3. Circle the kinds of shelter.

   house   nest   desert   cave   stable

4. Write the kind of shelter each animal uses.

bird	bear	dog	goldfish

5. Choose an animal. Tell about the animal's needs for food, water, and shelter. Then, make copies and share them with your classmates.

   _____

   _____

   _____

   _____

   _____

   _____

   _____

   _____

   _____

   _____

   _____

   _____

   _____

Name_____

1. What time is shown? _____

2. Count by 10s.

   430, 440, _____ , _____ , _____

3. Circle the box that has an odd number of tallies.

Read the song title. Rewrite the title with the correct capital letters.

1. "mary had a little lamb" _____

Read the sentence. Circle the helping verb. Underline the main verb.

2. Next week, I will sing in the school talent show.

Read the sentence. Add commas where they are needed.

3. My mother grows roses daisies and violets in her garden.

Draw a line to match each relationship with an example.

1. an animal helping a plant

2. an animal using a plant

3. a plant using a nonliving thing

4. an animal using a nonliving thing

A. A caterpillar eats a milkweed leaf.

B. A giraffe drinks from a watering hole.

C. A squirrel buries an acorn. It grows into an oak tree.

D. A sunflower grows in soil.

A government is formed to make laws and see that laws are obeyed. The government also protects the rights of the people who live in that country. It can also help people in need. The government works to keep order and discourage violence. Read each sentence. Circle **true** or **false**.

1. The government cannot protect your rights.   true   false

2. The government makes sure citizens are responsible.   true   false

3. The government discourages violence.   true   false

Rules and laws are necessary for countries to run smoothly. Countries would not be safe places to work and play without governments to make and enforce laws.

1. What do you think would happen if there were no traffic laws? Give reasons to support your opinion.

    _____

    _____

    _____

    _____

    _____

    _____

    _____

2. What do you think would happen if there were no police officers to keep people safe and respond to emergencies? Give reasons to support your opinion.

    _____

    _____

    _____

    _____

    _____

    _____

    _____

    _____

    _____

2.RI.3, 2.W.1, 2.L.1, 2.L.2, 2.L.3, 2.OA.C.3, 2.NBT.A.2, 2.MD.C.7 CD-104819 • © Carson-Dellosa

1. 8 – 5 = _____   9 – 7 = _____   11 + 6 = _____

2. 99 – 65 = _____   78 – 41 = _____

3. Write <, >, or = to make each statement true.

    451 ◯ 541   329 ◯ 309   25 ◯ 205

4. 34 + 12 + 40 = _____

Each day, the cat chased the mice. The mice had to hide. They could not hunt for food. They were hungry. "I know," said the smallest mouse. "Let's hang a bell around the cat's neck. Then, when we hear him coming, we can run."

1. Who are the characters in the story? _____

2. Why are the mice unable to hunt for food? _____

3. When you say **each**, how many sounds does **ea** have: one or two?

4. Which word could you use instead of **hungry**?

    A. full   B. starving

Circle where the parts are on a sunflower plant.

1. Where are the roots?   on a leaf   in the ground   on the stem

2. Where are the petals?   on a leaf   in the seeds   on the flower

3. Where are the seeds?   on a leaf   in the flower   in the roots

4. Where are the leaves?   in the flower   in the ground   on the stem

There are seven continents on Earth. They are Africa, Antarctica, Asia, Australia, Europe, North America, and South America. The United States is on the North American continent. Each continent has its own cultures, animals, and climates.

1. Name an animal you might see on the continent of Africa. _____

2. Which continent is the United States on? _____

3. How many continents are on Earth? _____

1. 5 + 7 = _____   3 + 6 = _____   4 + 9 = _____

2. 32 + 24 = _____   29 + 40 = _____

3. Write >, <, or = to make each statement true.

394 ◯ 394   721 ◯ 712   115 ◯ 15

4. The price of a toy is $12. I have $15. How much change will I get if I buy the toy? Write a number sentence to show how you got your answer.

   _____

5. Imagine you are the new owner of a toy store. What would you call the store? What toys would you sell? Show your completed story to a classmate. Make changes if needed.

   _____

   _____

   _____

   _____

   _____

   _____

   _____

   _____

   _____

   _____

   _____

2.RL.1, 2.RF.3, 2.W.5, 2.L.4, 2.NBT.A.4, 2.NBT.B.5, 2.NBT.B.6   CD-104819 • © Carson-Dellosa

Day 1

1. Jacob writes 27 letters while he is away at camp. He has 19 stamps. How many more stamps does Jacob need to mail all of his letters? _____ stamps

2. Write the number for each number word.
   three hundred fifty-six _____
   seven hundred twenty-one _____

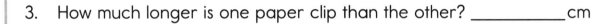

3. How much longer is one paper clip than the other? _____ cm

Day 2

Lisa hurried. She did not want to be late for her softball game. All of a sudden, wings grew on her back. She flew all the way to the field.

1. Circle the words from the story that rhyme with **new**.
   Underline the words that have two syllables.

2. Which word could you use instead of **all of a sudden**?

   A. quickly   B. suddenly

3. Underline the sentences that could not really happen.

Day 3

1. How does the life cycle of a mammal usually begin?
   A. The mother lays an egg.
   B. The mother carries her young inside of her.
   C. A seed is planted.

2. How does the life cycle of a plant usually begin?
   A. The mother lays an egg.
   B. The mother carries her young inside of her.
   C. A seed is planted.

Day 4

1. Draw a map of your school playground. Use a map key to label the items on it.

Heather woke up early. She picked up her new turtle. She named it Jewel because of the way its eyes sparkled.

"Good morning, Jewel," Heather said, petting her back. "Do you want lettuce for breakfast?"

"No!" Jewel answered. "I'd much rather have bacon and eggs."

1. Write each rhyming word from the story.

    blue _____   say _____   such _____

2. Which word could you use instead of **sparkled**?

    A. shone   B. watered

3. Could this story really happen? _____
    Underline the sentences that are not possible in the real world.

4. Write an ending to the story of Heather and her turtle Jewel. You can keep the story fantasy or turn it into real world.

    _____

    _____

    _____

    _____

    _____

    _____

    _____

    _____

    _____

    _____

    _____

    _____

    _____

    _____

    _____

 2.RI.3, 2.RF.3, 2.RF.4, 2.W.3, 2.L.4, 2.OA.A.1, 2.NBT.A.3, 2.MD.A.4   CD-104819 • © Carson-Dellosa

Day 1

1. Write the number 60 on the number line.

2. Miranda has 11 inches of border for the bulletin board. She needs 27 inches. How much more border does Miranda need to finish the bulletin board? _____ inches

3. 57 + 10 + 6 = _____

4. 674 – 124 = _____

Day 2

Many animals are called special names when they are young. A baby deer is called a fawn. A baby cat is called a kitten. Some baby animals have the same names as other kinds of baby animals. A baby elephant is called a calf. A baby whale is a calf. A baby giraffe is a calf. A baby cow is a calf.

1. What is the name of a baby deer? _____

2. How many baby animals are called calves? _____

3. What is the name of a young person? _____

4. Have you ever seen a fawn, a calf, or a kitten? _____

    Describe it. _____

Day 3

1. Look around your classroom at the other students. Complete the chart with traits about the students. Discuss your answers with a partner.

Different about each student	Same for everyone	Same for some of the students

Day 4

1. Draw a map of a room in your house. Use a map key to label the items in it.

Name_____

Use the chart to answer the questions.

Characteristic	Mom	Dad	Jorge
can wiggle earlobes	yes	no	no
brown eyes	yes	no	yes
long legs	no	yes	yes
left-handed	no	yes	yes

1. Can Jorge wiggle his earlobes? _____

2. Is Jorge left-handed or right-handed? _____

3. How many traits does Jorge have in common with his mother? _____

4. How many traits does Jorge have in common with his father? _____

5. Write about some of the traits you have in common with one of your parents or a relative. Tell whom you are most like. Describe how this makes you feel.

_____

_____

_____

_____

_____

_____

_____

_____

_____

_____

_____

_____

_____

2.RI.1, 2.RI.10, 2.RF.4, 2.W.3, 2.L.4, 2.NBT.B.6, 2.NBT.B.7, 2.MD.B.5, 2.MD.B.6

CD-104819 • © Carson-Dellosa

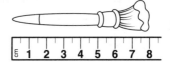

1. How long is the paintbrush? _____ cm

2. 14 + 23 + 41 + 19 = _____

3. Leigh caught 14 fish one morning. Later the same day, she caught 14 more fish. How many fish did Leigh catch in all? _____ fish

Day 1

Circle the letters that should be capitalized.

1. my friends and i went to the veterans day parade.

If the group of words is a complete sentence, color the fish purple. If the group of words is not a sentence, color the fish green.

2. Fish eat worms.

Add quotation marks around what the person said.

3. Jill won a medal, cheered the coach.

Day 2

Write **H** if the plant or animal lives in a hot habitat. Write **C** if the plant or animal lives in a cold habitat.

1. _____ rattlesnake   2. _____ cactus

3. _____ polar bear   4. _____ penguin

5. _____ arctic moss   6. _____ lizard

Day 3

Landforms can be near water such as coasts, harbors, and bays. Landforms can be raised areas of land such as mountains and hills. Lower areas of land, such as valleys and canyons, are also landforms.

1. Draw a landform that can be found in your city or state. Label it.

Day 4

Name_____

Look at the picture of landforms. Then, follow the directions.

1. Draw a fish in the lake.
2. Draw a dog beside the river.
3. Draw a whale in the ocean.
4. Draw a bird on the island.
5. Have you ever been to the coast or the mountains? Write about a landform you have visited and where it is located. Write about the things that you can do there. Use facts and definitions to explain your writing.

_____

_____

_____

_____

_____

_____

_____

_____

2.RI.10, 2.W.2, 2.L.1, 2.L.2, 2.OA.A.1, 2.NBT.B.6, 2.MD.A.1   CD-104819 • © Carson-Dellosa

Day 1

1. What number is 5 tens and 6 ones? _____

2. Write an equation for the array. _____

3. What unit would you use to measure a soccer field?

   A. centimeters   B. inches   C. yards

4. Jordan was selling frozen ice treats. Blake gave Jordan 2 quarters and 2 nickels. How much did Blake pay for the treat?
   _____ cents

Day 2

Kenan saved money all month. He wanted to buy a special gift for his grandfather. He bought a book about stereos. He knew his grandfather would love it.

1. Write the words that have three syllables. _____

   Which word starts with **st-**? _____

2. Cross out the word **gift**. Write another word for **gift**. _____

3. Could this story really happen? _____

Day 3

Write **T** if the statement is true. Write **F** if the statement is false.

1. _____ Soil is only one color.

2. _____ Soil can be made up of dead plants and animals.

3. _____ Different kinds of plants live in different kinds of soil.

4. _____ Soil can be made up of broken down rocks.

5. _____ Soil is only found in forests.

Day 4

1. Look at the two pictures. Compare and contrast the two places.

   _____

   _____

   _____

   _____

   _____

Name_____

1. What number is 6 tens and 4 ones? _____

2. Write an equation for the array. _____

3. What unit would you use to measure a TV?

   A. feet

   B. inches

   C. meters

4. Gabe went to see his favorite movie on Saturday afternoon. He gave the man at the ticket window 4 one-dollar bills, 5 dimes, 4 nickels, and 5 pennies. How much money did Gabe give the man at the ticket window?
   $ _____

5. How would you spend the money in Gabe's pocket if it were yours? If you are not sure how much something costs, look it up on the Internet. Or, ask your teacher or a classmate.

   _____

   _____

   _____

   _____

   _____

   _____

   _____

   _____

   _____

 2.RF.3, 2.RF.4, 2.W.3, 2.W.8, 2.L.4, 2.OA.C.4, 2.NBT.A.1, 2.MD.A.3, 2.MD.C.8

CD-104819 • © Carson-Dellosa

1. What unit would you use to measure the length of a ladybug?

   A. meters   B. centimeters   C. feet

2. What time is shown? _____

3. Write <, >, or = to make each statement true.

   16 ◯ 14   249 ◯ 429   90 ◯ 109

Circle the letters that should be capitalized.

1. julio went to wyoming last year for father's day.

If the group of words is a complete sentence, color the fish purple. If the group of words is not a sentence, color the fish green.

2. swims along the rocky shore

Add quotation marks around what the person said.

3. Hit the ball! Brian yelled to his brother.

---

1. What kind of living thing do you think each fossil was when it was alive?

   A.  _____   B.  _____

2. How do you know?

   _____

---

1. What are some ways to keep our Earth clean?

   _____

   _____

2. Draw a bumper sticker that would show people how to take care of our Earth and keep it clean.

1.   Circle the letters that should be capitalized.

     casey read *ramona the pest* over spring break.

2.   Read the words. If the words make a complete sentence, color the fish orange. If the words do not make a complete sentence, color it purple.

     The boat bobbed on the waves.

3.   Add quotation marks around what each person said.

     I pack my own lunch, I told my teacher.

     Good job! my teacher said.

4.   Circle the word that best completes the sentence.

     The (deer, dear) ran through the woods.

5.   Choose a partner. Together, write a short story about an imaginary conversation between a ladybug and a snail. One of you should write the words of the snail. The other should write the words of the ladybug. When you are finished, perform it for your classmates.

     _____

     _____

     _____

     _____

     _____

     _____

     _____

     _____

     _____

     _____

     _____

     _____

1. Kennedy has $0.92. Her sister gives her $0.08. How much money does Kennedy have now? $ _____

2. How many inches longer is one shovel than the other? _____ in.

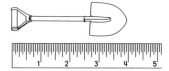 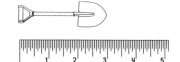

3. 87 + 13 = _____   91 − 35 = _____

Day 1

Squirrels eat nuts. Whales eat sea plants. Other animals eat many different things. A squirrel is hungry. He sees a pile of sea plants and a pile of nuts.

1. If you caught a squirrel, which word with **qu-** do you think would best describe the squirrel: quiet or squirmy? _____

2. What do squirrels eat? _____ What do whales eat? _____

3. Predict what the squirrel will do next. _____

   _____

Day 2

Circle each correct answer.

1. Which is taller?   hill   mountain

2. Which is smaller?   lake   ocean

3. Which is larger?   river   stream

4. Which is larger?   pond   lake

5. Which is smaller?   boulder   pebble

Day 3

Recycling, reducing, and reusing are all ways to keep our Earth clean. Reducing is cutting down on the amount of a resource we use. Write ways people can reduce the following:

1. water use _____

2. paper waste _____

3. plastic waste _____

4. energy use _____

Day 4

Name_____

1. Which is larger?   mountain   hill

2. Which is taller?   flower   tree

3. Which is longer?   creek   river

4. Which is larger?   pond   ocean

5. Which is higher?   hill   valley

6. Rocks and soil make up the earth we walk on. Think about a place where you have recently taken a walk or hike. Describe what you saw or felt. Use describing words such as **large**, **small**, **long**, **tall**, **short**, **heavy**, **light**, and others.

_____

_____

_____

_____

_____

_____

_____

_____

_____

_____

_____

_____

_____

_____

Day 1

1. What time is shown? _____

2. What unit would you use to measure a marker?

   A. feet   B. meters   C. centimeters

3. Write <, >, or = to make each statement true.

   50 ◯ 150   918 ◯ 98   51 ◯ 51

4. 333 − 222 = _____

Day 2

Dawn has been racing bikes every day after school for two years. She is tired of bike races. She wants to try something new. Dawn's teacher asks Dawn to swim on the swim team after school.

1. How long has Dawn been racing her bike? _____

2. How does she feel about bike racing now? _____

3. What decision does Dawn have to make? _____

   _____

4. What will Dawn probably do?

   A. Dawn will swim.   B. Dawn will race on her bike.

Day 3

1. Use adjectives to describe today's weather.

   _____

2. What do you think it will be like tomorrow?

   _____

3. Why?

   _____

Day 4

Economics is the study of how goods and services are produced and sold. Draw a line to match each word with its definition.

1. goods   A. things for sale

2. seller   B. work that people do for others for pay

3. produce   C. to make something

4. services   D. a person who has something for sale

Name_____

Look at the graph and data.

Strawberry

Mint

Chocolate

Vanilla

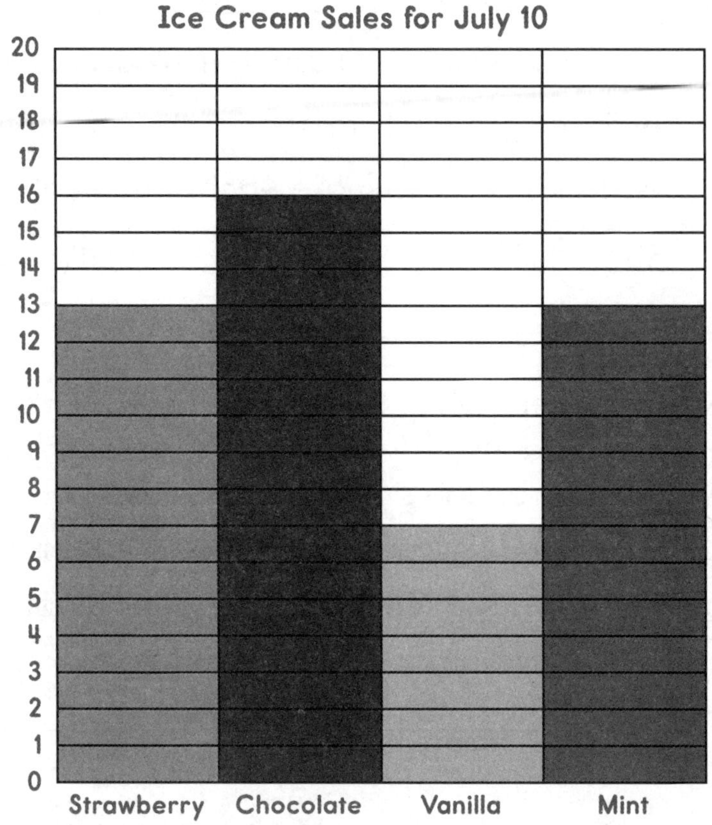

Ice Cream Sales for July 10

	Strawberry	Chocolate	Vanilla	Mint

(y-axis: 0 through 20)

1. Tell how the information in this graph would help the owner of the ice cream store.

   _____

   _____

2. What kind of business would be the best to own or to work for? Give reasons to support your opinion.

   _____

   _____

   _____

   _____

   _____

   _____

2.RL.1, 2.RL.3, 2.W.1, 2.L.1, 2.NBT.A.4, 2.NBT.B.7, 2.MD.A.3, 2.MD.C.7

1. Arianna was paid 2 quarters, 3 dimes, 4 nickels, and 5 pennies for an apple pie she sold at a bake sale. How much money did her pie cost?
$ _____

2. Write the number 70 on the number line.

3. Is the number of shaded squares even or odd? _____
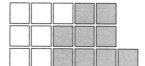

4. 786 – 231 = _____

Day 1

A long time ago, the sky was very close to the earth. When people were hungry, they just reached up and ate the sky. Sometimes, the sky tasted like beef stew, corn, or pineapple. Everyone was happy because they always had plenty to eat.

1. Which compound word has the **short a** sound in it? _____

2. What is the opposite of **plenty**? _____

3. Did this story really happen, or is it a fantasy? _____

Day 2

Use the words in the word bank to complete the sentences.

collects	condense	evaporates	precipitation

1. When the sun warms water, the water _____.

2. When the droplets are cool enough, they _____ into clouds.

3. _____ returns the water to the surface of the earth.

4. The water _____ in oceans, lakes, and rivers.

Day 3

When a product is scarce, there is not enough of it. If the demand for a product is high, the product could sell out.

1. Think about a time when something you or your family wanted was sold out.

What was it? _____

Did you finally get it? _____

Why do you think it sold out? _____

Day 4

1.   Write whether each number is **odd** or **even**.

6 _____   32 _____   47 _____   69 _____

2.   Write the number 70 on the number line.

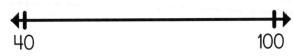

40   100

3.   772 – 451 = _____

4.   Rashad's lunch cost $1.40. He had $2.00 to spend. How much change did Rashad get back? _____ cents

5.   If you could buy anything on the school lunch menu, what would it be? List each item. Then, tell why you chose your meal plan. Type it on a computer or make a copy of it. If your teacher allows, show it to the cafeteria manager.

_____

_____

_____

_____

_____

_____

_____

_____

_____

_____

_____

2.RL.1, 2.RF.3, 2.RF.4, 2.W.2, 2.L.4, 2.L.6, 2.OA.C.4, 2.NBT.B.7, 2.MD.B.6, 2.MD.C.8

Day 1

1. There are 52 dogs walking in Central Park. If 19 of the dogs are barking, how many of the dogs are not barking? _____

2. 16 + 41 + 21 + 6 = _____

3. Add or subtract mentally.

   130 – 100 = _____   55 + 10 = _____

4. How long is the toy car? _____ cm

Write **there**, **their**, or **they're** to correctly complete the sentence.

1. It was _____ when I looked.

Use **or**, **and**, or **but** to join the sentences. Write the new sentence.

2. In his backyard, Juan found a cricket. Juan found a ladybug.

   _____

3. Read the envelope. Add the comma in the correct place.

   Chandra Park
   423 Center Street
   Bath Maine 89764

Day 2

Use the words in the word bank to identify the facts.

Earth	moon	stars	sun

1. _____ This star warms our planet.

2. _____ These objects group together to form galaxies.

3. _____ This object has many craters on its surface.

4. _____ This planet revolves around the sun.

Day 3

Write **N** if the item is a need. Write **W** if the item is a want.

1. _____ pet   2. _____ apple

3. _____ milkshake   4. _____ cake

5. _____ water   6. _____ milk

7. _____ candy bar   8. _____ bike

Day 4

1. Write **there**, **their**, or **they're** to complete each sentence.

    The swimming pool is over _____ .

    First, they will change _____ clothes.

    Then, _____ going to jump into the water.

2. Use **and**, **or**, or **but** to join the sentences. Write the new sentence.

    The dog found his bone. The dog found his red ball.

    _____

3. Read the invitation. Add commas in the correct places.

    > Come to My Party!
    >
    > Jonathan Chu
    >
    > Date: May 12 2015
    >
    > Place: My house
    >
    >   3133 Tonka Street
    >
    >   Telford Pennsylvania 18969

4. Plan a party. Think about the reason for the party. Whom will you invite? What will you do for fun? What will you eat? Write an interesting story.

    _____

    _____

    _____

    _____

    _____

    _____

    _____

    _____

    _____

    _____

2.W.3, 2.L.1, 2.L.2, 2.L.6, 2.OA.A.1, 2.NBT.B.6, 2.NBT.B.8, 2.MD.A.1

1. 272 + 13 = _____

2. Write <, >, or = to make each statement true.

   456 ◯ 564   112 ◯ 112   32 ◯ 23

Cookies Baked for the Bake Sale

Autumn ● ● ●
Spring ● ●
Summer ●

● = 10 cookies

3. How many more cookies were baked for the autumn sale than the spring sale? _____ cookies

---

Chin loves to count. She counts everything. She counts leaves. She even counts clouds. The math test is tomorrow. Chin practices counting and adding all evening.

1. Who is in this story? _____

2. Is Chin a boy or a girl? _____

3. What does Chin love to do? _____

4. How will Chin do on the test? _____

Write **T** if the statement is true. Write **F** if the statement is false.

1. _____ The sun is seen during the day.

2. _____ The moon is only seen at night.

3. _____ The moon is a light source.

4. _____ Without the sun, there could not be life on Earth.

When you save, you are putting away money. When you spend, you are buying things. Sometimes, people do not make good economic choices. You can plan a budget that will help you keep track of your spending.

1. What is one thing you want but do not have enough money for?

   _____

2. Write one way you can earn money to buy it. _____

3. Write one way you can save money to buy it. _____

Name_____

Use the words in the word bank to identify the facts.

| equator   moon   summer   sun |

1. _____ This is the warmest season because of direct sunlight.

2. _____ Light is reflected on this because of the sun.

3. _____ This can burn the skin if the skin is not protected.

4. _____ This is the hottest area of Earth because it receives the most direct sunlight.

5. Describe the things you do outside when the sun is shining. Then, describe the things you do outside when the moon is high in the night sky. What is the main difference? Which do you like best? Give reasons to support your opinion.

_____

_____

_____

_____

_____

_____

_____

_____

_____

_____

_____

 2.RL.1, 2.RL.3, 2.RF.4, 2.W.1, 2.W.8, 2.NBT.A.4, 2.NBT.B.7, 2.MD.D.10   CD-104819 • © Carson-Dellosa

1. Divide the circle into three equal parts.

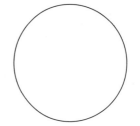

2. If 68 children signed up to play lacrosse and 74 children signed up to play soccer, how many more children signed up to play soccer? _____ children

3. Write the number for each number word.

six hundred fifty-five _____   nine hundred twelve _____

Write **there**, **their**, or **they're** to correctly complete the sentence. Circle each letter that should be capitalized.

1. _____ students in mr. hansen's class.

Use **or, and**, or **but** to join the sentences. Rewrite the sentence.

2. We might have pizza for lunch. We might have salad for lunch.

_____

Circle the best answer to each question.

1. Which is not an example of a system?
   A. a computer   B. a hammer
   C. the sun and the planets   D. your skeleton

2. What is the definition of a system?
   A. matter in an object   B. anything that takes up space
   C. a group of units working together D. things that are alive

---

Draw a line to match each word with its definition.

1. election   A. the leader of a state

2. vote   B. the leader of a city

3. elect   C. to make a choice

4. governor   D. to choose someone by voting

5. mayor   E. the event at which people vote

When a person decides to be a candidate for mayor, governor, or president, she must run a campaign. She may make radio and TV commercials that tell why people should vote for her. Candidates also make signs. The candidates want the most votes so that they can win the election.

1. Circle the words that show the character traits a candidate should have.

fair   dishonest   trustworthy

smart   lazy   unfriendly

2. Choose a person you think would make a good president. Give reasons to support your opinion.

_____

_____

_____

_____

_____

_____

_____

_____

_____

_____

_____

_____

_____

_____

_____

_____

Day 1

1. What time is shown? _____

2. 16 + 23 + 32 + 14 = _____

3. Count by 10s.

   750, 760, _____ , _____ , _____

4. Describe how this rectangle is divided. _____

Day 2

Jamie is a second grader who lives in the part of the United States that is known as the Midwest. He lives on a farm in Nebraska.

1. Who is in this story? _____

2. Is this person a boy or a girl? _____

3. What state does he or she live in? _____

4. Underline the best summary of this paragraph: Nebraska is in the Midwest or Jamie is a second grader from a farm in Nebraska.

Day 3

1. How might scientists work with other scientists using technology?

   _____

   _____

   _____

   _____

   _____

Day 4

The US president and his family live in the White House in Washington, DC. The president has many different jobs to do.

1. Name one job you think the president does. _____

   _____

2. Would you want to live in the White House? Why or why not?

   _____

   _____

Name_____

1. What time is shown?

_____

2. 21 + 13 + 32 + 12 = _____

3. Count by 10s.

340, 350, 360, _____ , _____ , _____

4. Describe how this circle is divided.

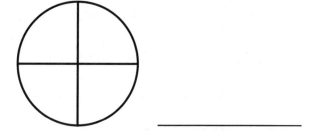

_____

5. If there were a rocket leaving for the moon today, would you get on it?
    Why or why not? Give reasons to support your opinion.

_____

_____

_____

_____

_____

_____

_____

_____

 2.RL.1, 2.RL.2, 2.RL.10, 2.RF.4, 2.W.1,
2.NBT.A.2, 2.NBT.B.6, 2.MD.C.7, 2.G.A.3

Day 1

1. Look at the bar graph. What night did the most people attend the play? _____

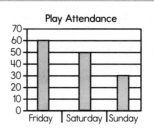
Play Attendance

2. Which unit would you use to measure the length of your finger?

   A. feet   B. yards   C. inches

3. Jenny is reading a book that is 98 pages long. She has read 47 pages so far. How many pages does Jenny have left to read?
   _____ pages

Day 2

Use proofreading marks to show correct capitalization and punctuation of the sentence.

1. linden had a party at super skate land How many people were at the party

Write **was** or **were** to correctly complete the sentence.

2. The children _____ putting on ice skates.

Day 3

1. Look around your classroom. What are three things that were made by people?

   _____ _____ _____

2. Choose one object. Tell what it helps you do.

   _____

Day 4

The United States has many symbols that represent it. There is the flag, the bald eagle, and the national anthem. Think about yourself and your family.

1. Draw the kinds of symbols that would best represent you or your family.

2. Choose one symbol and tell what it represents.

   _____

Name_____

1. Rewrite the sentence with the correct capitalization and punctuation.

   penny ran around and around her hamster wheel

   _____

2. Write **is** or **are** to correctly complete each sentence.

   The girls _____ doing a lot of homework.

   Gregory _____ one of the fastest runners.

3. Write **to**, **two**, or **too** to correctly complete each sentence.

   _____ squirrels ran up the tree.

   I like to dance _____ .

   Grandma will take me _____ the zoo.

4. Write a story about a friendship. Include how you met your friend and why you are still friends. Then, type the story on a computer and give a copy of it to your friend.

   _____

   _____

   _____

   _____

   _____

   _____

   _____

   _____

   _____

   _____

   _____

   _____

   _____

1. How many children voted for their favorite shape?

   _____ children

   Favorite Shapes

Square	☺
Circle	☺☺
Rectangle	☺

   ☺ = 5 children

2. Count by 10s.

   320, 330, _____ , _____ , _____

3. Taylor paid for her new necklace with a five-dollar bill. If the necklace cost $3.48, how much change did Taylor get back?

   $ _____

A **mantid** is an insect. We call it a praying mantis. When it hunts, it lifts its front legs and looks like it is praying. It has long front legs with sharp hooks to hold its prey.

1. Circle all of the words in the passage that have the **short a** sound.

2. What is a **mantid**? _____

3. What is this passage mostly about? _____

4. Use the information in the passage to finish this sentence. A mantid is called a praying mantis because _____.

How do scientists use the following math concepts?

1. addition _____

2. subtraction _____

3. measurement _____

4. graphing _____

Many countries celebrate their own independence days. These are days that symbolize freedom. The United States celebrates its Independence Day on July 4. On that day, flags are flown everywhere in celebration.

1. What does US Independence Day symbolize? _____

2. When is US Independence Day? _____

3. Write two facts about the American flag.

   _____

   _____

Name_____

1. Name three tools that can be used for science and math.

   _____   _____   _____

2. Large numbers are often used in science. Rewrite the numbers in numerals.

   Elephants may travel up to fifty miles a day to find food and water. _____

   Elephants may drink about two hundred twenty-five liters of water on a hot day. _____

   Elephants can live more than sixty-five years in the wild. _____

3. If a botanist plants 3 rows of 6 seeds in a small garden, how many plants will he have in all? Draw a picture to help you solve the problem.

   _____ plants

4. An inchworm looks like a small caterpillar. Use the Internet, books, and magazines to research and write a report about inchworms. Include interesting facts such as how the inch worm got its name.

   _____

   _____

   _____

   _____

   _____

   _____

   _____

   _____

   _____

   _____

   _____

2.RI.1, 2.RI.2, 2.RI.4, 2.RI.10, 2.RF.3, 2.RF.4, 2.W.2, 2.W.6, 2.NBT.A.2, 2.MD.C.8, 2.MD.D.10   CD-104819 • © Carson-Dellosa

Day 1

1. 521 – 295 = _____

2. Add or subtract mentally.

   350 + 100 = _____   540 – 10 = _____

3. Write the fraction for the shaded part of the shape. _____

4. Count by 5s.

   825, 830, _____ , _____ , _____

Day 2

Rewrite the sentences with correct capitalization and punctuation.

1. maria gonzalez gave lily a betty baby doll The doll had a yellow hat

   _____

Write **was** or **were** to correctly complete each sentence.

2. "She _____ skating fast," said Mariah.

3. The flowers _____ starting to grow.

Day 3

Fill in the missing letters.

1. Trees that are cut down for products such as p___p___r are often replaced with new trees.

2. After discovering a p___llut___d river, a group of students organized a cleanup.

3. Miners extract iron ore from under the g___ou___d.

4. When trees are cut down, animals often lose their ___o___es.

Day 4

Rural means having to do with country life. **Urban** means having to do with city life.

1. Name something you might see in the country. _____

2. Name something you might see in the city. _____

3. Name something you might see in the city and the country.

   _____

Read each sentence. Circle **rural** or **urban**.

1. Cows are eating grass in a field.

    rural   urban

2. Cars, trucks, and buses fill the streets.

    rural   urban

3. People live in apartment buildings.

    rural   urban

4. Corn is growing everywhere you look.

    rural   urban

5. Write about living in a rural or urban area. Tell about things you would do. Include facts and definitions to help you explain.

    _____

    _____

    _____

    _____

    _____

    _____

    _____

    _____

    _____

    _____

    _____

    _____

    _____

    _____

2.RF.3, 2.W.2, 2.L1., 2.L.2, 2.L.4, 2.NBT.A.2, 2.NBT.B.7, 2.NBT.B.8, 2.G.A.3

1. 47 + 56 = _____   84 − 15 = _____

2. Olivia has 98 coins in her bank. She gives away 17 coins. How many coins does she have left? _____ coins

3. Use the information to complete the line plot.

Distance Ridden on Bikes

      1 mile   = 7 people
      2 miles = 4 people
      3 miles = 1 person

```
  +--------+--------+
  1        2        3
```

Shannon dropped a marble. It hit the sleeping cat on the nose. The surprised cat jumped on the dog's tail. The dog yipped and chased the cat.

1. What happened first? _____

2. What happened second? _____

3. What happened third? _____

4. What happened fourth? _____

Use the words in the word bank to complete the sentences.

coal	nonrenewable	renewable	sunlight

1. Resources that do not run out are_____ resources.

2. An example of one is _____.

3. Resources that do run out are called _____ resources.

4. An example of one is _____.

Sometimes, you must make decisions all by yourself. Knowing what to do in certain situations can help you make good decisions and stay safe. Read the problem.

When coming home from school, you meet a woman who is crying. She says she has lost her puppy. She asks you to help her find it.

1. What is one thing you could do to solve the problem? Share your answer with a classmate. Does she agree or disagree?

_____

1. Use the information to complete the line plot.

   3 feet = 4 people

   4 feet = 6 people

   5 feet = 3 people

   Distance Jumped in Track and Field

2. 38 + 63 = _____

3. 146 + 327 = _____

4. Joey's mother placed 36 peas on his plate. Joey ate 18 peas. His mother placed 8 more peas on his plate. How many peas are on Joey's plate now? _____ peas

5. Write about a food you do not like to eat. Give reasons to support your opinion. How do you avoid eating it?

   _____

   _____

   _____

   _____

   _____

   _____

   _____

   _____

   _____

   _____

   _____

2.RL.5, 2.RF.4, 2.W.1, 2.L.4, 2.OA.A.1, 2.NBT.B.5, 2.MD.D.9

1. 471 – 382 = _____

2. Color the cubes.

3. Forrest scored 12 points during his Monday night basketball game. On Tuesday night, he scored 22 points. How many points did Forrest score in all? _____ points

Predators are animals that eat other animals. The animals they eat are called **prey**. Predators and prey do important jobs in nature. Prey animals are food for the animals that hunt them. But, predators also help prey.

1. What do you call an animal that eats other animals? _____

2. What do you call an animal that is eaten by other animals? _____

3. How does the prey help the predator? _____

    _____

Recycling is a way to change an item back into an earlier form of itself to make something new. **Composting** is a way to recycle food scraps so that they turn back into soil. Brainstorm the following:

1. items you can recycle at school

    _____

2. items you can recycle at home

    _____

You can keep track of important assignments, dates, school events, and after-school activities on a calendar.

1. Draw a calendar for this month.
    Write the correct dates.
    Fill in any activities you have for
    the month on your calendar.

My family went to the state fair this year. We had a good time. My favorite attraction was the Mega-Slide. The giant slide was 28 feet long. It was really tall. I was a little scared. But, I slid down anyway. It seemed to take forever to walk up the stairs to the top of the slide. But, sliding down was over in a blink of an eye. It was thrilling! I went down the Mega-Slide six times.

1. What is this story about?

    _____

2. What was the name of the special fair attraction in the story? _____

    _____

3. How did the writer feel about the slide? _____

    _____

4. Give reasons to support your answer to question 3.

    _____

    _____

5. Think of a ride or event you have attended at a fair or a carnival. Tell as much about it as you can remember. Explain why this was a special experience.

    _____

    _____

    _____

    _____

    _____

    _____

    _____

    _____

    _____

    _____

    _____

2.RI.1, 2.W.1, 2.W.8, 2.L.4, 2.OA.A.1, 2.NBT.B.7, 2.G.A.1

Name_____

1. Draw an array for the equation.

   5 + 5 + 5 + 5 + 5 = 25

2. Color the shapes that have 5 angles.

3. 27 + 42 = _____   49 – 37 = _____

Children around the world celebrate their birthdays in many different ways. In Argentina, people pluck the earlobe of the birthday child. They give one tug for each year the child has been alive. In China, family and friends eat noodles to ensure a long life. In England, people put objects in the birthday cakes. If a birthday child finds a coin, it means that she will be rich.

1. Circle all of the words in the passage that have **-ck** in them.

2. Which word means the same thing as **tug**: poke or pull? _____

3. Where is your **earlobe**?   A. top of your ear   B. bottom of your ear

4. How many tugs on your ear would you get on your next birthday? ____

Carl's cupcakes were too flat. He tried cooking them longer, but they burned. He added more baking powder, but they tasted bad. Carl conducted research and found that he might be over-stirring the batter. He made three more batches. He stirred the first batch for one minute, the second batch for five minutes, and the last batch for 10 minutes. After baking all three batches at the same time, the second batch was perfect.

1. How does Carl's work relate to science? _____

_____

1. Create a time line of your year at school. Include important dates and events such as field trips and special parties.

_____

Tony's class was learning about food and the human body. Mrs. Gupta asked the students what they ate for breakfast. Tony ate cereal and milk. Some students ate eggs, bacon, and toast. Other students ate breakfast cookies. A few students did not eat breakfast at all. The class voted on which breakfasts they thought were good choices. Mrs. Gupta asked the class to record their breakfast foods every morning for a week. Then, at 10:00 each day, she asked the students if they felt hungry. The class found that the students who ate good breakfasts felt better.

1. How does Mrs. Gupta's breakfast activity relate to science?

    _____

    _____

    _____

2. What did the students learn by the end of the week?

    _____

3. What did you eat for breakfast this morning? What are your favorite breakfast foods? Write an essay to answer these questions. Tell if you think these are healthful breakfast choices. Give reasons to support your opinion.

    _____

    _____

    _____

    _____

    _____

    _____

    _____

    _____

    _____

    _____

    _____

2.RI.1, 2.RI.4, 2.RI.10, 2.RF.3, 2.RF.4, 2.W.1, 2.L.6, 2.OA.C.4, 2.NBT.B.5, 2.G.A.1

Day 1

1. Write the fraction for the shaded part of the shape.

   _____

2. Write the number for each number word.

   four hundred thirteen _____

   three hundred sixty _____

3. 94 – 66 = _____   87 + 45 = _____

Day 2

A cat ran under a fish tank. The fish tank wobbled back and forth. Water and one small fish splashed onto the floor. The happy cat ate the fish. A thirsty dog lapped up the water.

1. What was the effect on the dog? _____

2. What was the effect on the cat? _____

3. What caused the chain reaction? _____

Day 3

Use the words in the word bank to complete the sentences.

| biologist   field work   forests   problems |

1. A _____ is a scientist who studies living things.

2. Some biologists work outdoors. This is called _____.

3. Some biologists work to save _____ or study sea animals.

4. Biologists need to learn to solve _____.

Day 4

1. Circle the kinds of transportation you have used.

2. How is traveling by train different from traveling by a car?

_____

3. Which is the fastest way to get to another continent? _____

Name_____

Vacation is a time when families may travel to a special place. They may visit special people.

1. Write about a time you and your family traveled to a special place for a vacation. Where did you go? What kind of transportation did you use? How long did it take to get there? What are some things you did while you were there? Include details to describe thoughts, feelings, or actions.

_____

_____

_____

_____

_____

_____

_____

_____

_____

_____

_____

_____

_____

_____

_____

_____

_____

_____

_____

_____

Answer Key

Page 9

Day 1: 1. 17 – 7 = 10; 2. B; 3. C;
Day 2: 1. the country; 2. her backyard;
3. Answers will vary but may include horses, cows, barns, vegetable gardens, sheep.
Day 3: 1. eat; 2. Clean; 3. mix; 4. Listen;
Day 4: 1. Answers will vary but may include school or park. 2. Drawings will vary.

Page 10

1. 26; 2. C; 3. 10, 12, 14; 4. C; 5. Answers will vary. 6. Stories will vary but should include details about a purchase and feelings.

Page 11

Day 1: 1. 8, 9; 2. 5 cm; 3. 1, 3, 5; **Day 2:** 1. The 2. (circled) cat, dog; 3. birds; **Day 3:** 1. hand lens; 2. timer; 3. calculator; 4. computer;
Day 4: 1. school; 2. the community

Page 12

1. Fruit, Turn, Yellow; 2. (circled) banana, hen; 3. skateboards, dinosaurs; 4. Answers will vary. Check students' punctuation.

Page 13

Day 1: 1. 37; 2. B; 3. 12 cents; **Day 2:** 1. (circled) each o/O in Otter, olives, octagons; 2. B;
3. October; **Day 3:** 1. balance scale, ruler, yardstick, stopwatch, thermometer;
2. Answers will vary. **Day 4:** 1. Answers will vary but should include appropriate classroom rules.

Page 14

1. Answers will vary. 2. Drawings will vary but should show the scale tipping to the side of the heavier item. 3. Answers will vary.

Page 15

Day 1: 1. 6 cm; 2. 21; 3. 22; **Day 2:** 1. Where; 2. (circled) cup; 3. gloves; **Day 3:** 1. Answers will vary but may include animals, plants, or rocks. 2. Answers will vary but may include to create smaller, more manageable groups.
Day 4: 1. future, past, present; 2. Answers will vary but may include dinosaurs.

Page 16

1. present, past; 2. Answers will vary but may include method of travel and clothes.
3. Answers will vary but should include valid reasons.

Page 17

Day 1: 1. four, ten, seven; 2. Drawings will vary. 3. 4 – 1 = 3 lollipops; 4. 5, 3, 6; **Day 2:** 1. sweet; 2. an animal that eats only plants; 3. calves;
Day 3: 1. Answers will vary but may include: Do cheeses melt at different temperatures? What cheese melts the fastest?
Day 4: 1. right, responsibility; 2. right, responsibility

Page 18

1. nine, twelve, eight; 2. 6; 12 – 6 = 6;
3. Drawings will vary but may include a circle or other figures without sides or angles.
4. Answers will vary but should include step-by-step instructions and number words. (Example: The dealer gives each player five cards.)

Page 19

Day 1: 1. 6 scoops; 2. <, <, =; 3. 62, 34, 30;
Day 2: 1. Mary Lou French, a tarantula;
2. venomous spider; 3. sandwich and chips;
Day 3: 4; 1; 5; 2; 3;
Day 4: 1. Answers will vary. 2. Answers will vary but may include that he planted apple seeds in the right places.

Page 20

1. green sea turtles; 2. It uses an egg tooth to chip its way out. 3. in the sand; 4. Reports will vary but should include details gained from research.

Page 21

Day 1: 1. 7 grapes; 2. <; 3. odd;
Day 2: 1. Marcus; 2. farms; 3. (circled) both;
Day 3: 1. Answers will vary but may include a T-chart or a picture graph.
Day 4: 1. dictionary; 2. atlas; 3. thesaurus

Page 22

1. Mrs. Garcia's class; 2. Mr. Lee's class; 3. 26;
4. Reports will vary but should include the correct steps of a butterfly metamorphosis (caterpillar, cocoon, butterfly).

Page 23

Day 1: 1. 68; 2. (circled) two rectangles, square; 3. 15 laps; **Day 2:** 1. (circled) t, n;
2.(underlined) eat; 3. Answers will vary, but end punctuation should be a question mark.
Day 3: 1. Answers will vary, but the adjectives should be underlined.
Day 4: 1. An Italian explorer; 2. Niña, Pinta, and Santa Maria

Page 24

1. Answers will vary. 2. Answers will vary but should include valid reasons.

Page 25

Day 1: 1. 59; 2. even; 3. 8:30;
Day 2: 1. newspapers; 2. jealous; 3. that she could be the biggest dog on the block;
Day 3: 1–3. Answers will vary.
Day 4: 1. Answers will vary but may include have a trusted adult or neighbor watch you for two hours. 2. Answers will vary but may include offering to help the classmate with his homework.

Page 26

1. 87; 2. even; 3. 10:30; 4. Answers will vary but should include reasons to support students' opinions.

Page 27

Day 1: 1. 80 + 3 = 83; 2. 5; 3. 28 – 16 = 12 flowers; 4. 11, 20; **Day 2:** 1. (circled) t, ?;
2. (underlined) hops; 3. watches;
Day 3: 1. solid, liquid, gas; Answers will vary for examples given: **Day 4:** 1. Time line should include the following dates: Born, 1962; Trained for first Olympics, 1981; Silver medal, 1984; Gold medal, 1988; Bronze medal, 1992.

Page 28

1. (circled) o, s, j ,a; 2. (underlined) swims, plays; 3. (underlined) x, mixes; sh, wishes; 4. Answers will vary. 5. Answers will vary but should show research from question 4. The story should include revisions, if needed.

Page 29

Day 1: 1. 5 cents; 2. >, >, =; 3. 7, 9, 6;
Day 2: 1. In a mouse house; 2. at midnight;

3. mice; 4. No, their ideas are impossible.
Day 3: 1. liquid; 2. ice, solid; 3. water vapor, gas; **Day 4:** 1. Plains, Southwestern, Eastern Woodland

Page 30

1. taste (or see), see (or taste), space, mass, forms, solid, liquid, gas (final three in any order); 2. Answers will vary but may include boiling water for tea, heating soup, melting an ice cube. Check for correct sequencing.

Page 31

Day 1: 1. 432, 204; 2. square; 3. 4 miles;
Day 2: 1. (circled) w, b; r, r; 2. P, C;
3. !; **Day 3:** 1. top; 2. push, down; 3. hill; 4. pull;
Day 4: 1. Inventing the telephone; 2. 1876; 3. Thomas Watson

Page 32

1. Graphic organizer should include: invented telephone, taught music, taught speech, created deaf research laboratory, invented electric probe, located icebergs using echoes. 2. Answers will vary.

Page 33

Day 1: 1. A; 2. 370, 380, 390; 3. 51, 79;
Day 2: 1. 4:00; 2. A; 3. in a submarine deep in the ocean; 4. octopus/animals of the deep ocean; **Day 3:** 1. o, e (force), a, t (Earth); a, i (floating); 3. Answers will vary but may include dropping an object.
Day 4: 1. Drawings and sentences will vary.

Page 34

1. A; 2. 270, 280, 290; 3. 88, 34; 4. 23;
5. Answers will vary but should include facts about a movie and conclude with a recommendation.

Page 35

Day 1: 1. Drawings will vary. 2. 35; 3. even;
Day 2: 1. (circled) m, g, l; m, a, n; 2. P, C;
3. .; **Day 3:** 1. magnet; 2. Earth; 3. compass;
Day 4: 1. Answers will vary. 2. Answers will vary.

Page 36

1. (circled) d, f; m, g, e; a, c; 2. P, C, P; 3. I am looking for my cat. Will you help me look for my cat? I cannot believe you found my cat! 4. Answers will vary.

Page 37

Day 1: 1. 5 + 5 = 10 or 2 + 2 + 2 + 2 + 2 = 10;
2. thirty, sixty-one, seventy-three;

3. ; **Day 2:** 1. sung; 2. not possible, cannot happen; 3. a loose tooth; 4. Answers will vary. **Day 3:** 1. B; 2. B; **Day 4:** 1. secondary; 2. primary; 3. secondary; 4. primary

Page 38

1. B; 2. (circled) sound, light, heat; 3. Answers may vary but may include heat, solar, and light; 4. computer, microwave, lamp, (Some students may circle cars.); 5. Answers will vary. If possible, have a computer available. If not, help students copy and share their work.

Page 39

Day 1: 1. ; 2. <, >, <; 3. 120, 630, 890;
Day 2: 1. *Green Eggs and Ham*; 2. (circled) can, (underlined) watch; 3. commas after math, history; **Day 3:** 1. vibrations; 2. soft; 3. high; 4. ears; **Day 4:** 1. January or February; 2. dragon; 3. watch fireworks

Page 40
1. fact; 2. opinion; 3. opinion; 4. fact;
5. Answers will vary but should follow the prompt.

Page 41
Day 1: 1. 200 + 30, 500 + 70 + 3; 2. Answers will vary. 3. 555, 148, 113; **Day 2:** 1. no; 2. Birds migrate south so that they can find food. 3. Answers will vary. **Day 3:** 1. B; 2. D; 3. A; 4. C; **Day 4:** 1. Answers will vary but may include that current phones have screens and are cordless.

Page 42
1. 400 + 60 + 6, 100 + 0 + 4; 2. 52, 538, 116, 336, 622; 3. 65; 4. Answers will vary but should include data from polling friends and revisions, if needed.

Page 43
Day 1: 1. 3 + 3 + 3 = 9; 2. 22 eggs;
Day 2: 1. *The Big Book of Lizards*;
2. (circled) will, (underlined) write;
3. (circled) can, (underlined) fly; 4. (circled) will, (underlined) rise; **Day 3:** 1. L; 2. N; 3. N; 4. N; 5. N; 6. N; 7. L; 8. L; **Day 4:** 1. Answers will vary but should include having the chance to do something you could not otherwise do.
2. France

Page 44
1. (circled) will, can; (underlined) ride, find; 2. *Dog Fancy*; 3. *The Horse That Spoke Spanish*; 4. Answers will vary.

Page 45
Day 1: 1. 96; 2. >, <, =; 3. Drawings will vary. **Day 2:** 1. Ellen and Avery; 2. B; 3. scared, frightened; **Day 3:** 1. plants; yes, yes, yes, no; animals: no, yes, yes, yes; 2. water and air; **Day 4:** 1. Check students' labeling.

Page 46
1. C; 2. B; 3. house, nest, cave, stable; 4. birdhouse or nest, cave, doghouse or home, fishbowl or aquarium; 5. Reports will vary. Help students copy and share their work.

Page 47
Day 1: 1. 8:30; 2. 450, 460, 470; 3. ;
Day 2: 1. "Mary Had a Little Lamb"; 2. (circled) will, (underlined) sing; 3. commas after roses, daisies; **Day 3:** 1. C; 2. A; 3. D; 4. B; **Day 4:** 1. false; 2. true; 3. true

Page 48
1. Answers will vary but should include valid reasons. 2. Answers will vary but should include valid reasons.

Page 49
Day 1: 1. 3, 2, 17; 2. 34, 37; 3. <, >, <; 4. 86; **Day 2:** 1. a cat and mice; 2. They are too busy running from the cat. 3. one; 4. hungry; **Day 3:** 1. in the ground; 2. on the flower; 3. in the flower; 4. on the stem; **Day 4:** 1. Answers will vary but may include lion, zebra, or giraffe. 2. North America; 3. seven

Page 50
1. 12, 9, 13; 2. 56, 69; 3. =, >, >; 4. $15 – $12 = $3; 5. Answers will vary.

     CD-104819 • © Carson-Dellosa

Page 51
Day 1: 1. 8; 2. 356, 721; 3. 4 cm;
Day 2: 1. (circled) grew, flew; (underlined) Lisa, hurried, softball, sudden; 2. B; 3. (underlined) All of a sudden, wings grew on her back. She flew all the way to the field.
Day 3: 1. B; 2. C; **Day 4:** 1. Check students' maps. Maps should include map keys.

Page 52
1. new, way, much; 2. A; 3. No, the last two sentences should be underlined. 4. Answers will vary.

Page 53
Day 1: 1. (number line showing 20, 60, 70); 2. 16; 3. 73; 4. 550; **Day 2:** 1. fawn; 2. 4; 3. kid, child, or baby; 4. Answers will vary.
Day 3: 1. Answers will vary but may include: Different: fingerprint; Same: have organs, breathe; Same for some: hair color, eye color. **Day 4:** 1. Check students' maps. Maps should include map keys.

Page 54
1. no; 2. left-handed; 3. one; 4. three; 5. Answers will vary.

Page 55
Day 1: 1. 8; 2. 97; 3. 28; **Day 2:** 1. (circled) m, i, v, d; 2. purple fish; 3. "Jill won a medal,";
Day 3: 1. H; 2. H; 3. C; 4. C; 5. C; 6. H;
Day 4: 1. Check students' drawings.

Page 56
1–4. Check students' drawings. 5. Answers will vary.

Page 57
Day 1: 1. 56; 2. 4 + 4 = 8 or 2 + 2 + 2 + 2 = 8; 3. C; 4. 60 cents; **Day 2:** 1. grandfather, stereos; stereos; 2. Check that students have crossed out gift; present; 3. yes; **Day 3:** 1. F; 2. T; 3. T; 4. T; 5. F; **Day 4:** 1. Answers will vary but may include that the Arctic is cold, and the desert is hot. Penguins, seals, and polar bears live in the Arctic, and lizards live in the desert.

Page 58
1. 64; 2. 2 + 2 + 2 + 2 + 2 + 2 = 12 or 6 + 6 = 12; 3. B; 4. $4.75; 5. Answers will vary.

Page 59
Day 1: 1. B; 2. 8:40; 3. >, <, <; **Day 2:** 1. (circled) j, w; f, d; 2. green fish; 3. "Hit the ball!";
Day 3: 1. A. leaf; B. insect; 2. Answers will vary but may include saw the veins of the leaf and the six legs and wings of the insect.
Day 4: 1. Answers will vary but may include picking up trash and recycling. 2. Drawings will vary.

Page 60
1. (circled) c, r, p; 2. orange shark; 3. "I pack my own lunch,"; "Good job!"; 4. deer; 5. Answers will vary. Provide ample opportunity for students to pair with others and then share their work.

Page 61
Day 1: 1. $1.00; 2. 1 in.; 3. 100, 56;
Day 2: 1. squirmy; 2. nuts, sea plants and animals; 3. He will eat the pile of nuts.
Day 3: 1. mountain; 2. lake; 3. river; 4. lake; 5. pebble; **Day 4:** 1–4. Answers will vary.

Page 62
1. mountain; 2. tree; 3. river; 4. ocean; 5. hill;
6. Answers will vary.

Page 63
Day 1: 1. 4:45; 2. C; 3. <, >, =; 4. 111;
Day 2: 1. two years; 2. She is tired of it.
3. to change from bike racing to swimming;
4. A; **Day 3:** 1–2. Answers will vary. 3. Answers will vary but may include how the weather will be similar to today's. **Day 4:** 1. A; 2. D; 3. C; 4. B

Page 64
1. Answers will vary but may include that the store should have more chocolate ice cream in stock than vanilla during the month of July.
2. Answers will vary but should include valid reasons.

Page 65
Day 1: 1. $1.05; 2. (number line: 30, 70, 90);
3. odd; 4. 555; **Day 2:** 1. pineapple; 2. Answers will vary but may include **none**. 3. fantasy;
Day 3: 1. evaporates; 2. condense;
3. Precipitation; 4. collects; **Day 4:** 1. Answers will vary.

Page 66
1. even, even, odd, odd;
2. (number line: 40, 70, 100); 3. 321; 4. $0.60; 5. Answers will vary but should focus on a meal plan.

Page 67
Day 1: 1. 33; 2. 84; 3. 30, 65; 4. 6cm;
Day 2: 1. there; 2. In his backyard, Juan found a cricket and a ladybug. 3. Bath, Maine; **Day 3:** 1. sun; 2. stars; 3. moon;

4. Earth; **Day 4:** 1. W; 2. N; 3. W; 4. W; 5. N; 6. N; 7. W; 8. W

Page 68
1. there, their, they're; 2. The dog found his bone and his red ball. 3. May 12, 2015; Telford, Pennsylvania; 4. Answers will vary.

Page 69
Day 1: 1. 285; 2. <, =, >; 3. 10; **Day 2:** 1. Chin; 2. girl; 3. count; 4. She will do well.
Day 3: 1. T; 2. F; 3. F; 4. T; **Day 4:** 1. Answers will vary. 2. Answers will vary but may include offering to do chores for neighbors.
3. Answers will vary but may include to not spend your allowance each week.

Page 70
1. summer; 2. moon; 3. sun; 4. equator;
5. Answers will vary.

Page 71
Day 1: 1. (circle with Mercedes symbol) ; 2. 6; 3. 655, 912;
Day 2: 1. They're, (circled) m, h;
2. We might have pizza or salad for lunch.
Day 3: 1. B; 2. C; **Day 4:** 1. E; 2. C; 3. D;
4. A; 5. B

Page 72
1. (circled) fair, trustworthy, smart; 2. Answers will vary but should include facts and definitions to explain.

Page 73
Day 1: 1. 1:40; 2. 85; 3. 770, 780, 790;
4. thirds; **Day 2:** 1. Jamie; 2. boy; Nebraska;
4. (underlined) Jamie is a second grader from a farm in Nebraska. **Day 3:** 1. Answers will vary but may include to share photos and facts and email each other.
Day 4: 1–2. Answers will vary.

Page 74
1. 2:25; 2. 78; 3. 370, 380, 390; 4. It is divided into four parts, or quarters. 5. Answers will vary, but opinions should be given with reasons.

Page 75
Day 1: 1. Friday; 2. C; 3. 51;
Day 2: 1. (capitalized) Linden, Super Skate Land; period after **Land**, question mark after **party**; 2. were; **Day 3:** 1. Answers will vary but may include a chair, table, or pencil.
2. Answers will vary. **Day 4:** 1. Symbols will vary. 2. Answers will vary.

Page 76
1. Penny ran around and around her hamster wheel. 2. are, is; 3. Two, too, to; 4. Answers will vary.

Page 77
Day 1: 1. 20; 2. 340, 350, 360; 3. $1.52;
Day 2: 1. (circled) mantid, mantis, an;
2. an insect; 3. the mantid; 4. it looks like it is praying when it hunts. **Day 3:** 1–4. Answers will vary. **Day 4:** 1. freedom; 2. July 4;
3. Answers will vary but may include that the flag has 13 stripes and 50 stars.

Page 78
1. Answers will vary but may include a thermometer, a balance scale, and a calculator. 2. 50, 225, 65; 3. 18; 4. Answers will vary.

Page 79
Day 1: 1. 226; 2. 450, 530; 3. $\frac{3}{4}$; 4. 835, 840, 845; **Day 2:** 1. Maria Gonzalez gave Lily a Betty Baby Doll. The doll had a yellow hat. 2. was; 3. were; **Day 3:** 1. a, e (paper); 2. o, e (polluted); 3. r, n (ground); 4. h, m (homes); **Day 4:** 1. Answers will vary but may include tractors and barns. 2. Answers will vary but may include traffic and tall buildings. 3. Answers will vary but may include people and pets.

Page 80
1. rural; 2. urban; 3. urban; 4. rural; 5. Answers will vary.

Page 81
Day 1: 1. 103, 69; 2. 81;

Distance Ridden on Bikes

3.  ; **Day 2:** 1. Shannon dropped a marble. 2. The marble hit the cat on the nose. 3. The cat jumped on the dog's tail. 4. The dog chased the cat.
Day 3: 1. renewable; 2. sunlight;
3. nonrenewable; 4. coal; **Day 4:** 1. Answers will vary but may include to tell the woman that he will bring an adult back with him to help her.

Page 82
Distance Jumped in Track and Field

1. ; 2. 101; 3. 473; 4. 26;
5. Answers will vary.

Page 83

Day 1: 1. 89; 2. Students should color two cubes. 3. 34; **Day 2:** 1. predator; 2. prey; 3. It is food for the predator.
Day 3: 1–2. Answers will vary but may include: 1. paper, plastic water bottles, and fruit and vegetable scraps (composted); 2. newspaper, empty food containers, and food scraps (composted); **Day 4:** 1. Calendars will vary.

Page 84

1. a trip to the state fair, the Mega-Slide; 2. Mega-Slide; 3. The writer first feared the slide but then enjoyed it a lot. 4. It seemed to take forever to walk up the stairs; the writer went down the Mega-Slide six times. 5. Answers will vary.

Page 85

Day 1: 1. Drawings will vary.

2. ; 3. 69, 12; **Day 2:** 1. (circled) pluck; 2. pull; 3. B; 4. Answers will vary.
Day 3: 1. Answers will vary but may include having a question to solve, trying different things to answer, and observing the results.
Day 4: 1. Check students' time lines.

Page 86

1. Answers will vary but may include having a question to answer, keeping various data over time, and coming to a conclusion based on the data. 2. They learned to choose a good breakfast. 3. Answers will vary.

Page 87

Day 1: 1. $\frac{2}{3}$; 2. 413, 360; 3. 28, 132;
Day 2: 1. The dog drank water. 2. The cat ate a fish. 3. The cat ran under the fish tank.
Day 3: 1. biologist; 2. field work; 3. forests; 4. problems; **Day 4:** 1. Answers will vary. 2. Answers will vary but may include that you cannot stop to visit many places when traveling by train. 3. by airplane

Page 88

1. Answers will vary.